The Very Heart of Worship
~ Knowing and Believing God Is ~

Written by
Cypress Ministries

Bible Study Series

The Very Heart of Worship

Copyright © 2011 by Cypress Ministries

All rights reserved. No part of this book may be reproduced or transmitted in any form or by any means without written permission of the author.

ISBN 978-0983413509
Published by Faith Books Publishing
www.faithbookspublishing.com
Spreading God's Word and the message He lays on the hearts of those who are called to do His work in writing.

Unless otherwise stated in this book:
Scripture is taken from the New Century Version®. Copyright © 1987, 1988, 1991 by Thomas Nelson, Inc. Used by permission. All rights reserved.

DEDICATION

This writing is dedicated to our heavenly Father
who so often reminds me to
"Be still and know that *IN ALL THINGS* I AM GOD."

To His Son, who is truly the Author and Finisher of my faith,
and it is in Him that I am able to find strength each day,

To His Holy Spirit who teaches me, leads me,
and tugs at my heart when I don't know where to go.

When I stumble with, "Who am I?"
the Lord picks me back up with,
**"Who has given man his mouth, and makes him deaf
or mute? Who gives him sight or makes him blind?
Is it not I, the Lord? Now go; I will help you speak
and will teach you what to say"**
(Exod. 4:11–12)

It is in Christ's name that I give all glory to God, who is the true
Author of these words that I have penned.
I give thanks to Him for I am simply a vessel and humbled
that each morning when I rise
He gives me a heart for His Word to write down.

And so with a trembling heart, I simply say, "Thank You, God."

Listen in your heart as the Lord whispers to you,
"All that you need... I AM."

Scripture says that God will create in us
a new heart and a new spirit,
and that He will prepare us to love
Him with all of our hearts.
(Scripture references: Ezek. 36:26 & Deut. 30:6)

At some point in your life,
the Lord will ask you to lay everything down
and simply worship Him.
His promise is simple:

"Come to Me, all you who are weary,
and burdened, and I will give you rest."
~Matt. 11:28~

He draws you, He calls you,
He says, "Come and see,"
and then He extends His hand
and invites you to come and get to know Him.

Table of Contents

INVITATION 1
LETTER FROM KASSIE 3
OPENING PRAYER 7
Part 1: KNOWING GOD IS 9
   To Know Him 11
   First Hand Knowledge 16
Part 2: BELIEVING GOD IS 27
   A Name To Know Him By 29
   God Is All-Powerful 35
   God Is All-Knowing 45
   God Is Faithful 53
   Section Break 1 63
   God Is My Liberator 69
   God Is My Guardian 77
   God Is My Guide 89
   God Is My Counselor 99
   God Is My Provider 107
   Section Break II 115
   God Is Loyal 119
   God Is My Teacher 125
   God Is Good 133
   God Is Truth 139

God Is My Friend 147

God Is Stable 157

God Is My Healer 165

God Is My Peace 173

God Is My Wisdom 179

God Is My Companion 185

The Living God 191

Section Break III 197

God Is My Deliverer 199

The Name of Jesus 209

A Worshiper's Heart 215

Part 3: Study Reference 221

Names of God Memory Verses 222

Core Study Chapter Nehemiah 9:5–25 224

Closing Prayer 227

About Cypress Ministries 229

About This Book 230

INVITATION

God's Word commands us to "love the LORD with all of our heart and mind." The Bible tells us that man looks at outward appearances, but that our Lord looks into our hearts. If we are to give God worship that is truly sincere and heartfelt, to offer our lives in a way that is pleasing to God as our spiritual act of worship, then we must first have an understanding of who God is to us. God calls and invites us to know Him personally. Our LORD God has many names and different characteristics. Each of us will know Him differently throughout various times and seasons in our lives.

Join us as we discover many different ways we can come to know God and who He is as we simply worship Him because **GOD IS**:

All-Powerful	Teacher	All-Knowing
Truth	Faithful	Friend
Liberator	Stable	Guardian
Healer	Guide	Peace
Counselor	Wisdom	Provider
Companion	Loyal	Living God
Good	Deliverer	

> "Praise the LORD!
> Praise Him, you servants of the LORD;
> praise the name of the LORD.
> The LORD'S name should be praised now and forever. The LORD'S name should be praised from where the sun rises to where it sets. The LORD is supreme over all the nations; His glory reaches to the skies."
> ~Ps.113:1-4~

LETTER FROM KASSIE

Dear Friend,

I don't know to whom I am writing this letter. I don't know who you are, where you live, or what your circumstances are like, but what I do know is that God does. I want you to know that I have prayed about you before ever starting this project and throughout writing this book. Though I don't know your face, you have been in my heart each step of the way. Please know that I have been asking God to lead me and praying that I would be a vessel He could use to share His message with you.

Several years ago, it became not enough for me to just read the Bible. I found myself hungry for a deeper understanding of God and His Word. So I started studying day in and day out. I found myself, like the Bereans, eager to hear what was said and then "study the Scriptures every day" (Acts 17:11) to find out for myself what the Word of God said.

At one point, on my knees in prayer, I found myself asking God, "Please, can I just have You? King Solomon asked for wisdom, and I need that also, but even more than that I desire to know You, not just about You. Lord, teach me to know You the way Abraham did, and face-to-face like Moses."

At another point I asked God, "Please, would You help me to know You with certainty and clarity. Lord, help me to know Your voice so that no matter where I am at or what's going on around me, when You say my name, when You whisper to me, I can say, 'Yes, Lord.'"

I am here to tell you that God heard me, answered my prayers, and took me at my word—so I have taken Him at His. And in doing so, I have learned so much about the God I believe in and worship. I believe God is who He says He is. I believe God can and will do what He says He will do.

I still have much to learn, and it will take a lifetime, but it is one I am willing to give. Have there been difficult days? Yes. Have there been seasons of grief and despair? Yes. I have found that when you pray, "God, please give me faith to walk on water," watch out, because there are going to be storms! But I have also learned to feel God's peace, which so surpasses any understanding that I could not even begin to explain.

I have learned that, in order to experience God and build a personal relationship with Him, He will indeed lead you through some very low valleys. But even now I can say that I am thankful for them, because they have made me so much more appreciative for the times when He picks me up and I am on mountain tops with Him. I believe that this is what I am supposed to share with you.

So here I am, to share what God has taught, and is still teaching me. I am here to be a witness to you that God is still God, He will always be God, and there is no other God. The same God before is our God now. If He will walk with me and help me and my family, then my friend, *know* that He will for you, too.

What I share with you in this book is based on things my family and I have personally experienced and learned from God in our lives. Again, please know I have prayed daily for God to lead me in writing this book so that it would not be just my message but what He would have me to say. In saying this, I encourage you to personally pray for God's wisdom and understanding. I am hoping and asking that you will take the time to look up Scriptures that I have suggested in your Bible and let God's Holy Spirit lead and teach you. I truly believe that if we seek Him with our whole hearts, He really does let us find Him.

One last note I would like to share: In doing my studies and research for this book I have used several different Bible translations and commentaries. However, my personal daily Bible, the Bible I pour over with love, sweat, and tears in my daily walk with God, is the New Century Version (NCV). It is this version that I have decided to use for Scripture quotes in this book simply because I have found that this is an easy version to understand when I am reading the Bible to my children or in Bible studies and counseling sessions with people who aren't as familiar with the Bible.

I believe the reason there are so many different Bible translations today is because God wants everyone to be able to understand His Word. In the same way that the sign over Jesus' cross was written in several languages so that everyone could read and understand it, we have many different Bible versions so that each of us can be taught and read God's Word in a language we can understand.

A friend of mine uses the New International Version (NIV). First John 1, in my personal Bible says, "We write to you…" But in her personal Bible, it says, "We proclaim to you…" which is very fitting for both of us. You see, I write, so in my Bible God's Word speaks to me in a language I totally get and I can understand it. And as for my friend? She teaches at women's community Bible studies and women's conferences. She "proclaims" using her voice, whereas I use a pen (okay, computer). But the same message from God's Word reaches both of us.

So, dear friend, in closing, if I don't see you face-to-face on this side of heaven, I will see you later when we both get there. But until then, may God bless, keep you, and smile upon you.

Sincerely,
Your Friend in Christ,
Kassie

OPENING PRAYER

Father God,

I don't know who is holding this book, I don't know who is reading this at the moment, but I praise You, God, because I know that You do.

Lord, I pray for this reader. I pray that should they decide to read this book and follow along with this study, which I believe You have put in my heart to share with them, that it will be a blessing and help them in their walk with You.

Lord, I am praying that each time this reader opens this book they will come here first and spend a quiet moment with You. Please help them to clear their minds of any distractions that would hinder them from learning from and hearing You in Your words. Father God, I ask that You would open their minds to perceive You, their hearts to know You, and their ears to hear You and Your message that You have to speak to them.

Lord, I truly pray that You will create in them a heart of worship that is pleasing to You. I also pray that by sharing my experiences and testimonies with them, it will help them to grow in their own personal relationship with You, so that they also will be able to bear witness to others that You alone are God.

In Christ Jesus' name I pray,
Amen.

Part 1: KNOWING GOD IS

"Then know and believe today that the LORD is God.
He is God in heaven and on the earth below.
There is no other God!"
~Deut. 4:39~

"God said to Moses, 'I AM WHO I AM.
When you go to the people of Israel,
tell them, I Am sent me to you.'"
God also said to Moses,
"This is what you should tell the people:
'The LORD is the God of your ancestors—
the God of Abraham,
the God of Isaac, and the God of Jacob,
He sent me to you.'
This will always be my name,
by which people from now on will know me."
~Exod. 3:14–15~

Then God said to Moses, "I am the LORD.
I appeared to Abraham, Isaac,
and Jacob by the name God Almighty,
but they did not know me by my name, the LORD."
~Exod. 6:2–3~

To Know Him

In the Bible, from cover to cover, God expresses His desire for His people to know Him. Listen with your heart as Jesus asks, **"I've been with you how long and you still don't know me…?"** (John 14:9). Recently, in a word search of three different Bible versions, the word "know" appears 1,244 times, and over 150 of those times it is God Himself declaring, "My People will know I am…"

In Psalm 81 God pleads with His people, **"Israel, please listen to me"** (vs. 8). Listen to the sorrow in God's voice as He says, **"But my people did not listen to me; Israel did not want me"** (vs. 11). God desires to be with us and to help us. **"I wish my people would listen to me; I wish Israel would live my way. Then I would quickly defeat their enemies and turn my hand against their foes"** (vss. 13–14).

In John 6, Jesus tells His followers that His people will be drawn to Him by God Himself and that He must not lose even one of them. Dear friend, please know that every time I sit down to write, I pray first. So if you are even slightly drawn to this book, if you are drawn to read the verses that I have suggested to you, then know that God is calling YOU, is drawing YOU, and wants a personal relationship with YOU. What He said to His people in Ezekiel 34, He says to YOU, **"You, my human sheep, are the sheep I care for, and I am your God, says the Lord God"** (vs. 31).

So many times in His Word, God assures us that whoever we need Him to be, then that is who God is. When we need comfort,

God is. When we need a guide, God is. When we need a provider, God is. Draw close to Him, listen to the strength and certainty in His voice as He speaks and says to you, "I AM GOD."

Imagine being a parent at your children's school waiting to pick them up. How would you feel if you were standing in view of them, just getting ready to say "Hello," and your child walked right past you? What if, as they were walking by, you heard them telling their friend, "I know I have a mom and dad, I just don't know which ones they are." I don't know about you, but I would be crushed if my own child didn't know who I was. But, that's what God has often experienced:

> **"I raised my children and helped them grow up, but they have turned against me. An ox knows its master, and a donkey knows where its owner feeds it, but the people of Israel do not know me; my people do not understand"** (Isa. 1:2–3).

Turn to Exodus 5:2: **"But the King of Egypt said, 'Who is the LORD? Why should I obey him and let Israel go? I do not know the LORD, and I will not let Israel go."** These were bold words! But he was going to see; he was about to know! God was about to introduce Himself. God was going to make it very clear that He was the LORD God. **"I will punish Egypt with my power, and I will bring the Israelites out of that land. Then they will know I am the LORD"** (Exod. 7:5). The Egyptians and Israelites weren't going to just learn something about Him. No, God said very clearly they were about to know Him.

When God brought His people out of Egypt, He gathered them together and said, **"I brought you here to Me"** (Exod. 19:4). He wants His people to be with Him, but He also wants His people to know Him personally. He says in Jeremiah 24, **"I will make them want to know Me, that I am the Lord."**

We have three boys, and the other day I did a load of laundry. When it was finished drying, I pulled it out and laid it neatly on the counter. Later, I went back and the pile was gone. It had been transported down the hall to the bedroom and for this I was pleased, until I saw what had happened to the load of clothes. The boys had taken the pile of clothes that I had laid out, which were ready to be hung up, and moved them from one place and stacked them in another. They were lying in a heap in the closet all wrinkled up! Now, when my kids went to wear them, the clothes wouldn't be as I had intended. Had the boys taken the time to hang them up, then when it was time to wear them, the clothes would have been nice and neat as I had wanted, but because the boys were in a hurry to do it their way, they missed out on what I had planned that was better for them.

God did the same thing with the Israelites. He took them out of Egypt, but instead of taking the road that would have gotten them to the Promised Land quickly; they took the long way around. God took the time to care for them and help them to become what He intended before giving them their new land. God could have easily picked them up, carried them over, and set them down, like the boys did with the load of laundry. The clothes were picked up, carried over, and set down in another heap with no time taken to care for them. If God had just picked the Israelites up and set them right back down in a new place, they would never have learned and experienced who God is and what God is capable of.

God does the same thing with us. When He liberates us, He could very easily set us right back down in a new location, but it wouldn't give Him the time to prepare in us what He would have for us. It wouldn't give Him time to change us, work in us, or allow us to experience Him in new ways.

When God liberates us, He will work in us to change our perspectives, our thoughts, our minds, and our hearts so that we can be prepared for the new things He wants to give us and do for us.

> **"I will give them a desire to respect Me completely, and I will put inside them a new way of thinking. I will take out the stubborn heart of flesh. Then they will live by my rules and obey My laws and keep them. They will be My people, and I will be their God"** (Ezek. 11:19–20).

Here is a thought: Last night, I baked a ham in the oven and used my cake pan. Today I want to bake a cake. I need to use my cake pan from last night, but I am going to clean it first before I create something new in it. I wouldn't just pull the pan out of the sink and use it. For one, that would be gross. But, more importantly, the cake would NOT come out appetizing nor would it taste the way it is supposed to. And I can tell you, my family would probably not want to eat it.

God wants us to know Him personally and experience things that only He can show us and learn things that only He can teach us. If we never had heartache, we would never know and appreciate the God who comforts us. We would miss out on how compassionate God is, and we wouldn't be able to teach this and extend His kind of comfort to others. If we never had struggles, then we would miss out on seeing God flex His muscles for us.

Have you ever seen the *The Three Musketeers*? My favorite part comes at the end when young D'Artagnan asks, "Now what do we do?" The reply is, "Well, we take care of the king and the queen." As the group is talking, an earlier adversary of D'Artagnan calls out to him, challenging him for a slight done to his sister. D'Artagnan says, "I'll take care of this." But before he can take a step, three swords block his path, and one of the three Musketeers says, "D'Artagnan, we also take care of each other!" And before he knows it, you hear the famous call, "All for one, and one for all." The next thing you see is a whole band of Musketeers running to confront D'Artagnan's challenger.

Our oldest son gets so annoyed with his younger brothers but, every once in a while when one of them is having difficulty, I will see my oldest son roll up his sleeves and say, "Here, let me."

When we come into the family of God, He also does this for us. God becomes our champion and our guardian. It's as if God says, "When they come after you, they come after me." God is ever so happy to be our shield and our strength, if we just let Him.

So many times we hear people say, *"Well, if there really is a God, then why..."* But just think, if we never have any need, we can't experience the pleasure of His incredible blessings. If we always have things go well for us, we don't learn to appreciate what God does for us. If life were always cake and ice cream we would miss out on seeing the very essence, the nature, of God.

Dear friend, if you are hungry for God, if you are hurting, if you feel like sometimes you are lost in an abyss and can't find your way out, just call on His mighty name. God promises to come after you. Jesus' crucifixion shows that He is more than able and willing to step into the very depths of hell to pull you out. He says, *"You are mine! You belong to me"*.

♥♥♥♥♥♥♥♥♥♥♥♥♥♥♥♥♥♥♥♥♥♥♥♥♥

Firsthand Knowledge

It isn't enough for us to know ABOUT HIM. We need to KNOW HIM. Last week my youngest son was invited to a birthday party—a little girl's birthday party. My son knows about her; he goes to school with her, knows about what kind of grades she makes, and how old she is turning. Not a whole lot of useful knowledge to get her a birthday present. So after discussing it, we decided to give money in a card that he handmade and she could buy something she wanted. It was not very personal, and I will admit not a whole lot of thought, or even effort, was put into this. The problem was we just didn't know her. Now, on the other hand, had it been the twins that are his best friends it would have made a BIG DIFFERENCE! We would have been at the store for a long time, going through all the different possibilities. "Oh! They would LOVE this," and "Hey, I know, how about..." or "They don't have THIS one..." I would have had to drag him out of the store, but we would have purchased and given them something they could really enjoy.

There is also a difference in knowing quite a bit about someone and really knowing them personally. I have a sister-in-law whom I love dearly, and we are pretty good friends. I could go some place and pick something out for her. Chances are she would like it and use the gift I give her. My brother, on the other hand, knows her personally in ways that I don't. So he is going to be able to pick out something much more personal.

In the same way, God wants us to know Him intimately and personally. If we don't have this kind of relationship with Him, it will be impossible to walk in faith with Him. If we don't allow Him to develop this kind of relationship in us with Him, we won't know when it is HIM talking to us and we won't be able to obey Him. If we don't know His voice and enjoy closeness with Him, we will spend all of our time arguing and questioning ourselves before stepping out in faith and following Him.

In First Kings, when Elijah stepped out and declared that it wouldn't rain again for three years and later, when he challenged the so-called prophets of Baal to a "duel," he had to have been extremely confident in who his God was, and that his God would back him up. Can you imagine how horrible it would have been if God hadn't come through for him? Can you imagine how devastating it would have been if, after Elijah boldly proclaimed, "It will not rain," then the very next day it did? Or what if in First Kings 18, after spending the whole day, taunting the Baal prophets, he said, "Now watch what my God can do..." and then nothing happened?

Elijah was certain he knew what God would do. He was also certain he knew what God was telling him to do. We, too, can have this kind of relationship with God. "But how?" you might ask. By allowing God to spend time with us (and in us). By allowing God to work in the recesses of our hearts, letting Him cleanse us, heal us, and change us in ways ONLY He can.

Our youngest son dropped a glass full of Kool-Aid in the kitchen a while back. It was an accident (not because he was horsing around) so I didn't get mad. The glass had shattered everywhere and red Kool-Aid was all over the floor. For the most part, I let him clean it up. But I was there to watch over him as I didn't want him cutting himself. He was pretty good at cleaning up what he could see, the obvious mess right in front of him. But, because this was NOT my first broken glass, I knew there was more of a mess than he could possibly see or even imagine.

I pulled out the refrigerator, and sure enough, there were glass slivers and red Kool-Aid. Had I not looked and taken care of it then come springtime, there would have been a bigger problem—ANTS.

I also moved the table back and under the legs there were slivers of glass. If I hadn't taken the time to look, then the first time one of the kids reached under the legs to get a toy they would have gotten a horrible surprise! Glass would have cut them. But, because I am older, I knew to look in places that our son wouldn't. He never would have thought the shattered glass could have sent pieces so far away. But, I did.

God's insight and wisdom is so much greater than ours. When God cleans house, He does a VERY good job. He cleans in areas we would never consider or even think of. You see, God knows so much more about us and so much more than we can possibly see. He'll go to the very root of things and past them, to places in our hearts we didn't even know were there. He will mend hurts that are buried so deeply that we've almost forgotten we pushed them there. But, during the cleansing, we are freed of our baggage and other stuff. And when we get to where He is taking us, we are prepared and changed in the process. It is so much different from when we first began. God gets us past ourselves to a place in ourselves that only He can touch. And somewhere along the journey we come to KNOW God.

The story of the Prodigal Son is very well known, and there are several lessons we can learn from it. But the lesson that touches me most is this: We all have different pressure points. Each of us has different breaking points. What may bring one person to their knees may have no effect on someone else. But what I have learned is: if God cannot get our attention quietly, He will do so in a way that we can't help but give Him all of our attention!

The other night, our kids were in the living room playing their Xbox. I wanted them to stop their game and come eat. I called for them but got no response. So I called for them again, this time a little bit louder but still got no response. So the THIRD time I went and stood in front of the TV (after turning it off) and with a much louder voice said, *"Please stop your game and come eat!"* You can bet I had their attention, but in a way that WAS NOT comfortable for them.

I think God does the same thing with us. He quietly calls for us, then knocks a little louder. But if He can't get our attention in a calm manner, He will let us start experiencing pressures in our lives, until sometimes we are literally on our knees. I admit I am very stubborn and don't like to give up or quit! So sometimes, even when on my knees, I refused to give in. It took A LOT for me to finally get to the point, on my knees and face down, of hearing God whispering, "Have you had enough?" When I think back about different times in my life, I wonder how often God whispered, "Have you had enough?" But I was too stubborn to back down. The incredible thing is, when you finally reach that point and you hear this soothing, "Have you had enough?" if you will just have the courage to say, "YES!" then you will hear a sigh as if God is saying "Finally!" And then you will hear Him say, "All you have to do is come home."

He will lift you up and help you begin the journey home to the place in life He wants you to be. He doesn't promise that there will never be pressures, difficulties, or heartaches. But He does promise that He will be with you through each of them. You will begin to experience a peace of heart and mind when you do go through tough times. You will find that even when rough things happen, there will be other things that will bring smiles and happiness that will help these rough patches not to be so noticeable or painful after all.

God is able and very willing to do so much *for* us and *in* us if we will only let Him. But we have to take that first step in accepting His invitation to us. We have to allow ourselves to dare to believe there is someone capable of so much more than us. We have to dare to believe there is someone bigger than us that we can't see with our naked eyes. We have to dare to believe there IS A GOD and that He wants a relationship with us. We have to dare to believe He cares for us. And the only way to know and believe this, is to spend time with Him, as it says in Ezekiel 36:27–28:

**"I will put my Spirit inside of you...
and you will be my people and I will be your God."**

I truly believe God longs for us to know Him personally and not just from someone else's viewpoint. There are so many different characteristics of God, so many different names by which to know Him. Who God is to me may not be the side and nature of God you see. Each day, we are on different walks, you and I. Each day, we are going to have different needs. The incredible thing about God is that He is a BIG GOD. So as He meets my needs today as my Provider, He may be meeting your needs as your Healer. *But He is still GOD.*

♥♥♥♥♥♥♥♥♥♥♥♥♥♥♥♥♥♥♥♥♥♥♥♥♥

One time when Jesus was praying alone, his followers were with him, and he asked them. "Who do the people say I am?" They answered, "Some say you are John the Baptist. Others say you are Elijah. And others say you are one of the prophets from long ago who has come back to life." Then Jesus asked, "But who do you say I am?" Peter answered, "You are the Christ from God" (Luke 9:18–20).

I think that must have made Him smile. For one, because of His statement, "Who do you say I am?" As if saying, "Ok, that's who they think and what they say, but what about YOU?" And when Peter said "He was Christ," I think that might have made Him smile. Maybe His thought was, "Finally, someone gets it!" In fact, in other parts of the Gospels Jesus told Peter he only knew that because it was what God Himself had shown him. And I think that must have pleased God very much. Peter believed what GOD HAD REVEALED instead of basing his opinion on what everyone else said.

Suppose you are getting ready to take a quiz and have 99 people telling you the answer is A. You can hear 99 people say, "Trust me, the answer is A." You can have 99 people trying to convince you, "The answer is A, and here's why." You can have 99 people saying it, but something inside just doesn't seem right. You know that 99 people are positive they are right, but somehow you find there is no peace. So you take the time to just think and listen and in the quietness of your heart—in the most peaceful recesses of your spirit—you hear a very solid whisper, "The answer is B." You come to a point where you have to decide, are you going to believe 99 people or are you going to believe God? But before you can learn to recognize that voice and know and trust that it's God's voice inside you, you have to KNOW GOD, and how He sounds to you— inside of you.

You can have so many people say, "You are..." You can have so many people giving their own opinion of you and who they think you are. You may have people forming and spouting off all kinds of thoughts about you. But you know what, my friend? You are who GOD SAYS you are. You may be going through some tough times and maybe people are beating you down. Everyone may have a thought about who they think you are, who you couldn't possibly be, or what you couldn't possibly do, but you know what? You are who

GOD SAYS you are. And God says you are "His people." God says, "He loves you." And God longs for YOU to know HIM.

Perhaps one of the most heart-wrenching verses in the Bible to me (besides Christ's crucifixion, and Peter's denying him) is:

> **"After Jesus said this, many of his followers left Him and stopped following Him. Jesus asked the twelve followers, 'Do you want to leave, too?' Simon Peter answered him, 'Lord, who we would go to? You have the words that give eternal life'"** (John 6:66–68).

After being fed in such an incredible way, after seeing so many things that Christ had just done for them, half the people there decided to walk away from Him. When I read this verse about Jesus turning and asking, "Do you want to leave, too?" my heart always hurts. Listen to the sorrow in His voice: *"Do you want to leave, too?"* Peter's response is the same as mine would be: "Where would we go?"

I can't imagine the rejection Jesus must have felt as He watched people He cared about, people He was willing to die for, walk away from Him. They just didn't get it. He had fed them, healed them, and befriended them, but they totally missed that the greatest gift He wanted to share with them was Himself (see John 4:16)!

If I were to give you a gift and it was in a big box wrapped up with a big bow, you could take it out of my hands, and even say, "Oh, thank you." But if you just take the gift from me, set it in your house somewhere and never open it up, you would totally miss what was inside. Sometimes I think that's what these people did.

We have a young son who is a dinosaur freak! He loves everything about dinosaurs and has lots of them. I keep telling him that one of these days we need to get them all out, put them together in herds, and count them to see how many he has. Last Christmas, we found a large T-Rex that he did not have. So, we got it for him, and wrapped it up and put in under the tree. After that, you should have seen the longing in his face every time we walked past one at the store. Boy, how he wanted one so much! It hurt me to see the look on his face, but I already knew he had one waiting for him at home.

It got even more painful when he had enough money of his own and wanted to buy one. Then he couldn't understand why, even with his own money, we wouldn't let him get one. Again, I knew he already had one. It was just waiting to be unwrapped. Those few weeks dragged by ever so painfully. He longed for that dinosaur so much. Now think if you will, how disappointing it would have been if he had just accepted the box it was wrapped in and said, "Thank you so much," and then never opened it. The thing he longed for the most would never have been received and he would have gone for months (and maybe for him, years) longing for something he had within his grasp—yet he just needed to accept what was being given to him on the inside! Something I knew he wanted so bad, and I was dying to give to him, would have just been left unopened and rejected because he hadn't bother to look inside. Of course, he did open it and the look on his face was priceless! He was thrilled, and so was I.

God longs to give us the very thing we need the most, Himself. But it comes from the inside. When we truly accept Christ, His Holy Spirit comes to live inside of us. It is also on the inside of us that God will work and build His relationship with us.

Everything those people in John 6 could have ever wanted or needed was standing right before them. Jesus was offering them the bread of life, a gift from the inside, and they turned it down. They walked away because they thought it would be too difficult. What they didn't realize, like so many people today, is that it's life without Christ that's difficult.

In First Samuel 8, Samuel was upset because the nation was calling for a king and he felt like they had rejected him. The sadness comes when God says *"No, they didn't reject you, they rejected me."* Look these verses up in your Bible; let the Holy Spirit touch your heart. Listen to God as He shakes His head and says, "No, they have rejected me." Listen with your heart as Jesus turns around and asks, "Do you want to leave, too?" Then look at the cross. Look at what God Himself offers each one of us. Then listen to Him as He asks you, "Do you want to leave, too?"

God will do so much for us, God will go so far for us, and God will take 99 steps for us. He just asks each of us to take one. God loves us, God calls to us, God wants us to know Him, but He won't force Himself on us. He waits for each of us to accept His help, His invitation.

When each of our boys was learning to ride their bikes without training wheels, we would run right beside them. They would wobble, twist, and turn almost to the point of falling down. We would go right alongside of them, sometimes with our hands stretched out, just waiting for them should they say, "Help!" Sometimes if there was a major wobble we would reach out and give them a little balance that they weren't even aware of. But, being "big boys," they didn't want our help. They wanted to do it by themselves. We were still right there, willing, but we weren't going to push our help on them. Granted, they eventually learned how to ride their bikes so well that the things they can do on their bikes scare me!

But friend, we aren't trying to ride a bike and God isn't trying to teach us to go without training wheels. He wants to walk with us every day, every step of the way. He longs to draw us close to Him so we can know Him personally and enjoy a close, intimate relationship with Him that will last always.

God says,
"I Am who I Am."

♥♥♥♥♥♥♥♥♥♥♥♥♥♥♥♥♥♥♥♥♥♥♥♥♥♥♥♥

I encourage you to read and listen as God says:

**"I am merciful, I am the One who heals you,
who comforts you,
and who answers your prayers."**
(Jer. 3:12, Exod. 15:26, Isa. 51:12, and Hosea 14:8)

Jesus said that He and the Father are one and He is the bread, the light, the door, and the resurrection. He is the way, the truth, and the life (John 6:35, John 8:12, John 10:9, John 11:25–27, and John 14:6). Every day, however you need Him, every way, whoever you need Him to be—all you could ever want or need, dear friend, <u>*GOD IS*</u>.

*Won't you please accept His call
to get to know Him, not just about Him,
and find out personally who He is and
who He will be for you?*

Part 2:
BELIEVING GOD IS
_____

"I am the LORD your God,
who stirs the sea
and makes the waves roar.
My name is the LORD All-Powerful."
~Isa. 51:15~

A Name To Know Him By

All that I am, praise the Lord; everything in me, praise his holy name. ~Ps. 103:1~

From the very beginning when God first started creation, He gave it a name. It wasn't enough for Him to just create something without a distinct name. **"God named the light 'day' and the darkness 'night.' Evening passed, morning came. This was the first day"** (Gen. 1:5). In Genesis 2, Scripture tells us that after God made man, He brought the animals and birds to man so he could name them. Several times elsewhere in Scripture when He gave someone a new life, He started by giving them a new name. And, when He was ready to rescue His people and called Moses to lead them, He began by introducing Himself so there would be no doubt about who was doing the talking! You can know about someone without knowing their name. But when you really get to know them, then you will also know their name.

When you know someone's name, your relationship becomes more personal than when they are just a face. That is what God wants us to do. He's GOD, yes. But when we spend time with Him, when we get to know Him, we find that—as if that weren't enough—He becomes so much more to us. He becomes personal to us, not just some lofty figure out there. God desires a personal, close relationship with us. He will even go to great lengths to introduce Himself to us. When we draw close to Him, He Himself will give us a name by which to call Him. It is so amazing that the God who created the universe wants us to be on a first name basis with Him!

The word "name" appears in the NCV Bible over 400 times. My favorite of these verses is:

> **"I am the Lord your God,**
> **who stirs the sea and makes the waves roar.**
> **My name is the Lord All-Powerful."**
> (Isa. 51:15)

When we have a very personal relationship with God, and come to know Him by name, then we can worship Him with much more intensity. When we praise God, it allows our hearts and our minds to become focused on who He is and not on ourselves and who we are.

Nehemiah 9:5–25 will be our core study passage in this second part of our book. This one passage shows us many characteristics of God and His nature. It gives us names by which to begin our relationship with God. Throughout the Bible God reveals Himself to us in many different ways and by many different names. Whereas I might use the name and say, "God is my Strength," you might use the name and say, "God is my Power." Two different names, both equally strong; still one God. We just have different languages.

But to help begin our journey, I would like to start by focusing on just a few names that God reveals as being His. I would also like to suggest that, as we start to explore different names by which to praise God, you keep a notebook of some sort. I am very much encouraging you to look the verses up in your own Bible and listen with your heart. Ask the Holy Spirit to open your mind and your heart and help you to hear God's voice as He speaks to you from His own words.

As God begins to introduce Himself to you personally, write the names down that He shares with you and the passages that the Holy Spirit lights up in you. I am encouraging you to keep a journal, to share with your family and friends, of the different verses in His Word that He opens up as He shows you, *"This is who I AM!"*

Why is it so important to write it down and share it? Because when we don't, we tend to forget, and then our children don't learn and won't be able to pass it down to their children. In Joshua 24:3, it talks about the fact that the Israelites served God as long as the elders who had witnessed God's hand were living. But as these leaders died, the lessons became fuzzy until they weren't spoken about anymore or even taught. Everyday life and other peoples' beliefs started dominating them, until God's beloved children had forgotten and turned away from Him. In fact, we are commanded to write it down!

> **"Write these things for the future so that people who are not yet born will praise the LORD."**
> (Ps. 102:18)

I started a small notebook and put orange tabs in it, labeling them with the key names that I was learning during my personal Bible study. When I came to verses that spoke strongly to me about who God is I would write them down. Now, with much enjoyment, I can pick up my notebook and meditate on verses that speak of God's name, which He has given me for my personal relationship with Him. In a second, larger notebook, I use a purple pen to rewrite these Scriptures down, and then with a black pen I journal a short note on how and why it is significant to me.

Later, I use a red pen to record things that happen over the next few days that confirm what God has revealed to me. Last, I use a blue pen to write down my thanks to God for speaking to me, showing me His will, and revealing Himself to me.

Part 2: Believing God Is

You might think it's pretty colorful, but when I look back at my journal, I can quickly and clearly see a difference between God's Word (purple ink), my prayers (blue ink), and God's handprints in my life (red ink).

In our first set of core study verses in Nehemiah 9, we will look at verses 5–8. In this first introduction of who God is, we will see God's greatness as being: *All-Powerful, All-Knowing, and Faithful.*

Core Study Verses Nehemiah 9: 5-8
"The People's Prayer"

**"Blessed be your wonderful name.
It is more wonderful than all blessing and praise.
You are the only LORD. You made the heavens,
even the highest heavens, with all the stars.
You made the earth and everything on it, the seas and
everything in them; you give life to everything.
The heavenly army worships you.
"You are the Lord, the God who chose Abram
and brought him out of Ur in Babylonia
and named him Abraham.
You found him faithful to you,
so you made an agreement with him to give
his descendants the land
of the Canaanites, Hittites, Amorites,
Perizzites, Jebusites, and Girgashites.
You have kept your promise,
because you do what is right."**

Please keep in mind that Nehemiah 9:5–25 will be our core study verses; however, we will be looking at several other verses during each name study, so, I suggest putting a colored sticky note in your Bible marking Nehemiah 9 to make it easier to turn back and forth. Ready?

Let's start by praying, shall we?

♥ **PRAYING IN FAITH**

Father God, thank You for this time You are giving us. Thank You for bringing us together to read Your Words and to study different ways in which to know You. I pray that You will help us to learn more about You. I pray that You will help this reader to know You more intimately as we begin to study Your Word. Lord God, with my heart, I pray that this reader, whoever they may be, will come to discover the message that You would have for them. Father God, I am praying this reader's heart will be touched in a very personal way, and that the words that You would have for them, the words that You would speak to them, will be made clear.
Thank You.
In Christ Jesus' name I pray,
Amen.

> "I am the LORD your God, who stirs the sea and makes the waves roar. My name is the LORD All-Powerful."
> ~Isa. 51:15~

God Is All-Powerful

God is a BIG GOD! The same God who told the ocean, "you can only go this far and no further," is our God. When He introduces Himself, He does it to leave no doubt. He is not the "dog with a loud bark but no bite." Sometimes when I read about God being all-powerful, I envision a mountain lion roaring.

God is omnipotent, meaning *all-powerful, almighty.* **"Then I heard what sounded like a great many people, like the noise of flooding water, and like the noise of loud thunder. The people were saying, 'Hallelujah! Our Lord God, the almighty, rules'"** (Rev. 19:6). It is so incredible that this same God, over and over in Scripture, says He is YOUR God. He didn't create you to only abandon you and let you battle life alone. If you have a need for something stronger than you, then you only have to call on the Lord God All-Powerful, because He is there ready and waiting for you. No matter what you are facing, the same God who created the heavens is more than strong enough to help you.

In the first part of our study of Nehemiah 9, starting with verse 5, we are reminded of our need to praise Him as we are introduced to the God who was able to create the heavens and the earth and everything in it.

<u>Core Study Verse Nehemiah 9:5</u>
"Blessed be your wonderful name.
It is more wonderful than all blessing and praise."

When we come to obstacles in our lives, we have an All-Powerful God who is more than able to roll up His sleeves and move mountains for us. When you come to a boulder in the road that takes up the whole path—you can't see over it, you can't see past it, and you can't see under it—then look up! There is a God who says, "I can take care of this." Take comfort in the strength of a God who says, **"Be still and know that I am God"** (Ps. 46:10).

There is nothing that we can come to in life that God is not able to help us face. **"I am God; I am the beginning and the end"** (Isa. 48:12). There is nothing too big that God cannot help us with. Yes, there are times when the prayer of "Help!" seems to go unanswered. Sometimes we have to just trust that God can see the bigger picture. Sometimes the "help" we are praying for may not be the best for us.

A few years ago I was without a job when I saw an ad in the paper, and applied for it, knowing I was very qualified. They needed help; I needed a job. So it was very frustrating when this job opportunity I thought I wanted kept being stalled. On my knees, I kept praying, "God, please help." But the help didn't come. Almost two months went by, that job was not coming to pass and neither were other ones that I had inquired about. Then, out of the blue, I got a phone call and was hired at a place I had known nothing about.

But I am so glad it came to pass, because shortly thereafter, my car broke down and the mechanic where I now worked was able to fix it for nothing! A few months later, pipes broke in my house and flooded the whole place. But because of where I was working, a subcontractor was able to come out to fix all of it, for very little. If I had been working anywhere else, these events would have been devastating, but because of where I was at I had the "help" I needed. I believe God heard my prayers for help months earlier, but He knew that the real "HELP" I needed was yet to come, so He waited.

God Is All-Powerful

I can only imagine the challenge they must have felt when the Israelites left Egypt only to be faced with a massive sea. I think God must have smiled a little bit as He was preparing to reveal a path they couldn't see. It's almost as if God's answer was "Hey, if I can lead you to it, then I can certainly lead you through it." God is able to make waters (our difficulties) part for us, and I think He takes great pleasure in showing us. But what is also incredible about God is that if we come to problems which, in His infinite wisdom He decides NOT to move for us, He promises to go through them with us. Read in your Bible the passage of Isaiah 43. Take comfort that God says when we go through waters, when we go through fire, *He will be with us.* He doesn't just say, "Well, do the best you can, and I will see you on the other side."

Take heart that the LORD God All-Powerful is strong enough to get us through them. Notice He does say it is a matter of *when,* so apparently it is to be expected that trouble will come. But also notice He uses the word *"through,"* which means it won't last forever. Even when hardships come in abundance and trials seem to take forever there still is the other side waiting for us, because God has promised.

Turn in your Bibles to Luke 1:36–38. When it was time for our Savior to come, the angel Gabriel told Mary that God can do anything. Jesus told His followers that nothing was impossible for God. (Read Mark 10 and Matthew 19.) When God was getting ready to bless His people, He told them in Zech. 8:6, **"This is what the LORD All-Powerful says: 'Those who are left alive then may think it is too difficult to happen, but it is not too difficult for me.'"**

Sometimes (most times) when God gives us an assignment, we may be excited and very willing and immediately say, "Okay." Then the enormity of it hits us. We realize how impossible it is for us and our strength, means, or resources, so we back up and say, "But God, I can't." God smiles and says, "It's okay, because I can." He just needs a willing vessel to be His arms and feet. He knows we are human, so He tells us, **"You will not succeed by your own strength or by your own power, but by my Spirit"** (Zech. 4:6). He just asks us to believe in Him, to trust Him, and to obey Him. Then watch, amazingly, as He accomplishes it through us.

Not only can the Lord God All-Powerful move mountains for us and help us through trying times, He can also give us victory. At times when we need Him to just step in and take over, He will.

A few years ago, our oldest son was in a three-day wrestling tournament for the middle school he attended. He is tall and lanky but strong. It was the end of the season in his first year of wrestling, and he had trained hard all season long. The first night of the tournament his name was drawn for the first match. The opponent my son was wrestling was bigger, and you could tell he had a few more years of experience than my son. All I could think when he was going out on the mat was "This is NOT going to be pretty." For three minutes I watched my son hold this guy off and keep himself from being pinned by the muscles in his neck! The other guy had him down, but our son decided he WAS NOT going to lie down. Our son decided in his heart "I may be beat this match but it will be by points, not by pinning." Our son used his neck muscles to keep his shoulders from touching the mats. While I was watching this all I could think of was how much his neck was going to hurt. Sure enough, when it was over my son came over and was moving his head side to side—trying to work the pain out—and said "Boy, Mom that hurt." My reply was, *"You think?"* So I gave him some medicine

The Very Heart of Worship

> God Is
> All-Powerful

and was really thankful he didn't have to compete again until the next day.

However, the next morning he was pulling his shirt over his head and came in saying, "Mom, I've never noticed my ribs sticking out like this before." That's because they never had! We took him to the doctor and were told he had probably cracked his ribs. His response was, "But I can still wrestle, right?" The doctor kind of laughed and said, "No, if the ribs were cracked you could puncture a lung or something worse." My son was devastated and concerned for the team since they were already short some members and he didn't want them losing more points because he would have to forfeit.

We were sent to the hospital to get x-rays. They had to take them three times because of all the swelling. While we were waiting for the results my cell phone rang. It was the doctor asking us to come back to his office; the x-rays had already been sent to him and he needed to see us.

So back to the doctors we went. Once there, the look on the doctor's face was my first clue that I was not going to like this. He grinned, kind of laughed, and just shook his head. Then he proceeded to tell us that our son had managed to rip every muscle off his rib cage and that the swelling was from all the blood. However, he DID NOT break any ribs. Again, my son's response was, "Can I wrestle?" I kept asking him, "Doesn't it HURT?" He informed me that it did, but the pain medication the doctor had given him earlier was keeping it at bay. I was in the process of telling him that in no way was he wrestling when, to my utter dismay, the doctor said he could. It is a good thing I know this man because my "WHAT?" wasn't very pleasant.

Being an ex-jock, he could sympathize and understood the whole "not wanting to forfeit. He told us our son had unfortunately pretty much done all the damage the doctor had hoped to avoid. He wasn't going to promise that there couldn't be any further damage, but he felt that our son had already done his worst. The doctor said that if our son didn't take any more pain medication (so as not to be too numb) and if he was wrapped, he could go out on the mat and attempt to compete so the loss would be less than the forfeit. But only if our son thought he could handle more pain, because by evening time he was probably going to be hurting. As much as it killed ME, we told him we would support whatever he decided but he had to decide soon because we had to let the coaches know. My concern was not only whether this was going to be extremely painful for him but that, if the other opponents could tell he was wrapped, they would go in for "the kill."

I took him to eat and, on a whim as we were headed back to the school, (he was starting to look kind of shaky about this) I asked him if he wanted to stop at a friend's church since we were right by it. I was pretty surprised when he said yes. We stopped and went inside. I walked with him as he went all the way up to the front and just sat down on the floor. His head tilted down and he started really shaking. I remember leaning down and whispering, "You know it's okay to be scared and its okay to back down. Whatever you decide is all right. You see that cross up there? God can hear you. God is listening to you and can help you decide." I also told him we could sit there as long as he needed.

After that I took a half step back and knelt down beside him and waited. I have no idea what conversation my son had with God that day. He has never told me. I have no idea what was said between his heart and God's. All I know is the transformation I watched in him. I watched him go from shaking and trying hard not to break down and cry, to relaxed, and then peaceful. Then his shoulders straightened up, his chest puffed out, and he looked up at me. Given the incredible look of certainty on his face, all I could do was say,

The Very Heart of Worship

> **God Is All-Powerful**

"Okay," and I knew that between him and God, *their* decision was made.

I took him back to the gym, where by then the team was getting ready to leave. We had already called to tell the coaches what had happened and that he was still going to wrestle. The head coach, a big burly guy, came over and leaned over my son in his BEST efforts to intimidate him into not participating said, *"If you so much as flinch, I will throw in the towel!"* My son just looked him straight in the face and told him he wouldn't have to. I had to laugh over the coach just shaking his head. I heard him mutter, "Where did you get this kid?"

That night, I sat in the stands and watched as he wrestled not only once, but twice! Yes, of course he lost, but he didn't just lie down and let it be a pin. He actually went for a bit each time and was able to get a few points. At the end of the tournament his team took fifth place. We had several people come up saying, "Hey, I thought he was hurt?" But you would have never known it. And more importantly his opponents didn't know either!

I cannot tell you how incredibly thankful I was to God. He truly was our God All-Powerful for my son that day. Not only did God give him comfort and strength, He gave him peace of heart and peace of mind. God completely filled him with His presence. He had to have because the transformation I watched in my child could only have been from God. I know it was God out there on the mat with him, God watching over him, God helping him, and God strengthening him to do something my son could not have done on his own. And in the end God gave my son victory. He may not have won the matches, but he was able to compete, finish the tournament, even score a few points, and was there for his team. But, I believe the victory was still there—INSIDE. And I am truly thankful.

Part 2: Believing God Is

I would like to leave you with one more mental picture of the Lord God All-Powerful in case you are still wondering who this God is that Nehemiah was praising and worshiping in our core study passage of Nehemiah.

Core Study Verse Nehemiah 9:6
"You are the only LORD. You made the heavens, even the highest heavens, with all the stars."

I like to close my eyes and picture Nehemiah as he stood there that day before the people and praised his Lord and God. How inspired he must have been to be able to voice such loving words.

Even though his words are touching, when I am in need of someone much more powerful than I am, I like to meditate on Psalms 77. Turn and read with me verses 14–19.

> **"You are the God who does miracles; You have shown people Your power. By Your power You have saved Your people, the descendants of Jacob and Joseph. God, the waters saw You; they saw You and became afraid; the deep waters shook with fear. The clouds poured down their rain. The sky thundered. Your lightning flashed back and forth like arrows. Your thunder sounded in the whirlwind. Lightning lit up the world. The earth trembled and shook. You made a way through the sea and paths through the deep waters, but Your footprints were not seen."**

How is that for an All-Powerful God? *The deep waters shook! The earth trembled!* I don't know about you, but that's enough for me! And, since we are descendants of Jacob, what He did for them, He will indeed do for us!

In closing of God is All-Powerful,

♥ **PRAYING IN FAITH**

Father God, we praise You for being our Lord God All-Powerful. Lord God, thank You for this time that we have shared studying Your Words that You have given us. Lord God, thank You for whomever is reading this with me at this moment, and I pray that You will bless them and show them that You are an Almighty God. Lord God, thank You for this opportunity to share with this reader the awesomeness of You.

Lord, we praise You because without fear, we can come to You with our difficulties and burdens. Thank You for the battles You fight, the obstructions and barriers You break down, and the mountains You move for us. Lord, we praise You because what would seem too difficult for us is never too difficult for You. Lord, You are God over heaven and earth, and we thank You because we know that it is by Your strength, not ours, that victory comes.

Father God I pray that this reader will be blessed by You, helped by You, and come to know You as their Lord God All-Powerful.
In Christ Jesus' name I pray,
Amen.

The Very Heart of Worship

> "Two sparrows cost only a penny, but not even one of them can die without your Father's knowing it."
> ~Matt. 10:29~

God Is All-Knowing

It started with one man. God, in His infinite wisdom, wanted to create a nation to show generations to come that *He is God*, so He had a plan. **"God began by making one person, and from him came all the different people who live everywhere in the world. God decided exactly when and where they must live"** (Acts 17:26). Just think, no matter where you are living right now, there is a reason and it serves a purpose even if you don't see it or understand it. It doesn't matter if things are or are not going well for you—know you didn't get there by yourself. There is a reason why you were born the year you were. Even if someone tells you that you were an accident, YOU WEREN'T.

In verse 7 of our study of Nehemiah 9, we are told that God chose Abram then took him out of where he was living and gave him a new name. But notice that first God chose the man He wanted. Throughout the Bible we read that God CHOOSES who He wants to lead His people and then He sends him. God chose Abram, and then He sent him to live where God needed Abram to be. Next, He gave Abram a new name. He didn't tell Abram, "Hey, I'm going change a few things." Nope, that wasn't nearly enough for our Lord. He told Abram, "You are going to become a whole new man."

<u>**Core Study Verse: Nehemiah 9:7**</u>
**"You are the Lord, the God who chose Abram
and brought him out of Ur in Babylonia
and named him Abraham."**

That is something so wonderful about God—when He decides to clean a person up, He does a very good job. Have you ever noticed how often the word "completely" is used in the Bible? "Completely destroy them..." and "Obey me completely..." God doesn't do anything halfway. When He forgives you of your sins, He also forgets them and erases them until they are no more. (Read Isaiah 43:25 and 44:22.) When God delivered any of His people out of bondage it was completely! Even though you won't see some of it on this side of heaven, rest assured that whatever work God is doing in your life He will complete His work in you. Dear friend, wherever you are at this moment, wherever you are in this stage of your life, whatever your circumstances are, whatever your situation is, GOD KNOWS.

Do you know the story of Zacchaeus? He wanted to see Jesus so badly that he was willing to climb up a tree when he couldn't see over the crowd. (Read Luke 19:1–7.) Nothing was going to stop Zacchaeus from seeing this Jesus everyone was talking about. But what I really love about this story is that Jesus KNEW where Zacchaeus was! As Jesus was coming down the street, Zacchaeus shimmied up the tree and was perched on a branch overhead. When Jesus got below where Zacchaeus was, Jesus LOOKED UP! Jesus knew this man would be up there in this tree and that this man's heart was ready to receive Him. So, when Jesus got to him, He looked up and called to him. Not only did Jesus call for him, but Jesus called Zacchaeus by name! Now keep in mind, no one had introduced them. But Jesus knew where he was and who he was.

My friend, I have news for you: He knows where you are and He knows your name, too. When I read this passage in Luke 19, I often wonder, could Jesus have taken another route? Is it possible the whole reason Jesus took this particular route, at that exact time, was to find this one man Zacchaeus and give him a personal invitation to salvation and a heavenly home? Jesus looked past what others perceived of this man and into his heart then gave Zacchaeus

> **God Is All-Knowing**

forgiveness, a second chance, and a new beginning. In the same way, He looks at you, calls you by name, and gives you a personal invitation. God does not change. Take to heart that in the same way God sent Jesus to find this man Zacchaeus, God will send Jesus to find you.

If you look back at our core study of Nehemiah 9:7, we see that God chose Abram. God had a plan for Abram. God knew who Abram was, but even better, God knew who Abram could, and eventually would, be. God also knew exactly at what point it was time to set His plan into motion.

When you think about the timing in Abram/Abraham's life, our All-Knowing Father, in His infinite wisdom, had a purpose and a reason for when He revealed His intent to give Abraham a son, and then waited until His timing was perfect to prove faithful and deliver what He had promised. Could God have given Abraham a son earlier in life? Of course, but I think He waited for two reasons: (1) to teach us that He could perform a miracle and show us that it didn't matter what the circumstance were like, and (2) because He knew at what point in time there would be a pretty young girl going to get water at a well.

God is all-knowing because if Isaac had been born earlier he might not have needed a wife at the time Rebekah would be going to the well. Isaac would have been older and at a different stage in his life and may not have waited, but instead married someone else earlier. However, in God's all-knowing wisdom He knew when to give Abraham and Sarah their long-awaited son, which put Isaac at the right time in his life for Abraham to send his servant out looking.

Hence, Abraham's servant arrived at the well in time to pray for God's guidance (see Genesis 24) and was there ready to meet Rebekah. My friend, not only is God all-knowing, but He can set things into motion to turn out at just the perfect time. What's sad is that so often these days, God's perfect timing is passed off as "coincidence." But this was no coincidence. Rebekah might have thought she was going to get some water, but what she probably didn't know was she was about to make a God-given appointment.

My friend, I don't know where you are at in your life, but take to heart that God does and can get you where you need to be—sometimes without you even knowing it. Just think, the same God who knew how to align the stars knows how to arrange events in your life to work out at just the right time and in ways that can often amaze us if we will just take a step back and look at the traces of His handiwork.

In the story of Ruth, she couldn't have understood at the time that God still had huge plans for her. All she knew was that she had lost her husband and her mother-in-law was planning to go home; Ruth couldn't stand to lose her, too.

In Ruth 1, Naomi, in her grief, decided to return to her family's home. In her despair, she thought God had forgotten her and that her life was over. In fact, she told her family not to call her Naomi anymore because that meant "happy or pleasant." Naomi told her family they should call her "Mara," because this meant "sad." Can you relate? Have you ever been at a point in your life where you just thought, "This is it, there can't be anymore, this is all there is"? Guess what? It wasn't "all she wrote" for either of these women. God still had a whole other book written out for them. Both of these women's lives had only just begun. And yours has too.

The Very Heart of Worship

God Is All-Knowing

I will admit that it was very sad for both these women, but God wasn't done. He set into motion a move, a meeting, and a baby! God gave Ruth a whole new life! And God gave Naomi a grandson, but not just any grandson. God wrote these two women right into Jesus' heritage. At the same time Naomi was crying sad and bitter tears and Ruth's whole world was shaken up as she was trying to figure out what to do next, God's will was already being done.

Dear friend, never underestimate your all-knowing, all-powerful, all-loving God. Don't ever think, "Well, that's it, my life is done, and this is just how it is." When you come to God, when you turn in your despair to God, He can do amazing things with the next chapter of your life. God knows where you have been and where you are at, but He also knows all you can be and all He can do in your life. It doesn't matter what you may think about yourself or what other people may say about, or even to you. It doesn't matter what your circumstances look like now, or how desolate your situation may seem, God can do amazing things in the heart of anyone who is willing to believe and turn to Him. How do I know that? How can I have the gumption to say that to you? Because, dear friend, God made you!

> **"You made my whole being;**
> **You formed me in my mother's body...**
> **All the days planned for me were written in Your book**
> **before I was one day old."**
> (Ps. 139:13, 16)

I smile as I write this because I can only imagine what some of you are feeling right about now. Have you gotten a little dinged up? Okay, if you are anything like I was, maybe a lot dinged up? It doesn't matter! You may not be in the original condition God intended. Again, it doesn't matter. When we come to the end of our rope and we are out of hope and in spiritual need, emotionally hurt, or maybe just plain ol' worn out, ask God, "What do YOU want for me? What would YOU have for me? What do I do now?" God smiles and probably looks at the angels and takes a sigh of relief as if to say, "Finally." Then He looks down at where you are at and gently says, "Here, let me."

In Psalm 139, in different versions of the Bible, the term "knit" is used. I love that because knitting takes both hands! It's not something you can do one-handed. When God first created us, He knit us together. It is so amazing to know that when God first made the sun, the stars, and the water, He spoke and it happened. But when it came time to create humans, He decided to use both of His hands. He wanted to be "hands-on" and involved in our creation.

Someone might be thinking, "But you don't know what I have done, what mistakes I have made." Friend, it doesn't matter. So many times in the Bible God says, "Return to me." It doesn't matter how much dirt and grime you may have waded into because God knows what is in the deepest recesses of your heart. You can't fool God, even if you wanted to. When you are truly sincere, then no matter how far you have fallen, God says, "Return to me."

Have you ever known someone who left home, went as far as they could go and then the bottom fell out on them and they made that phone call? They called with, "I don't know how I got here and I don't know what I was thinking. I just want to come home, but I don't know how and I don't have any money."

They may feel horrible, but you are just so relieved and happy to hear from them that all you can do is say, "Stay where you are, don't move, I WILL COME AND GET YOU." My friend, that's how God feels about you. Again, God does not change. He is the same God yesterday, today, and tomorrow. What He said to His people in

> God Is
> All-Knowing

Jeremiah 31:3, **"I love you people with a love that will last forever,"** He says to you.

If you read about Rahab in Joshua 2, you will see she was a prostitute! Did God condone her lifestyle? Of course not! But God already knew that when push came to shove, and when given the chance, deep in her heart was a belief and a desire for Him. She went from being a prostitute to being grafted into the family tree of our Savior.

She may have been a fallen woman but she showed her true heart. She took a chance and dared to believe what she had heard about God. Why do I say her "true heart"? Because she showed humility and compassion to others. When Joshua's men were getting ready to leave for battle, she asked them to **"Please remember and show kindness to my family."** It wasn't "me, myself, and I." She truly believed God would give the Israelites victory over Jericho. She believed God would do what He had said He would do. Then, she showed love for her family. What makes it humbling is that it wasn't about her. It wasn't, "Please save me or please remember me." No, it was "my family." I think God must have honored her for that. I think God must have looked beyond what was in her past and further than her current situation, and knew that in her heart she would choose Him. There was humility and sincerity in her, and throughout the Bible God shows that He will always respond to those traits.

My friend, I encourage you to take comfort in the fact that God is truly all-knowing. God had a plan from before He ever said, "Let there be light." Jesus was always God's plan for bringing us to Him. Jesus was God's redemptive plan before Satan ever asked Eve, "Did God really say...?" Jesus was not an accident or a plan that just came about as humanity went along. Nothing has ever taken God by surprise. God has never had to say, *"Well, let me rethink this,"* or

"Hmm, I wasn't expecting that, so now let's do this." God had a plan for Abraham and knew well in advance what Abraham's response would be. He already knew what would happen to Naomi's family as well as what Rahab's decision would be when the spies came to see her. Dear friend, God has plans for your future, too. (Read Jeremiah 29:11–14.) He knows where you are, where you need to be, and how to get you there. Don't give up hope; call out to God. Return to Him, sincerely give God a chance, and then just wait and see.

In closing of God Is All-Knowing,

♥ PRAYING IN FAITH

Father God, I don't know who I am praying with, but I praise You Father God because You do. We thank You, Lord, because without worry we can look to You, the one that knows all of our todays and tomorrows, and that You know where we should go and how to get us there. Lord, we praise You because we can trust that You have already prepared us for our journey. Lord, help us to stay focused on You, help us to see Your leading, and keep us in the center of Your perfect will for us.

Lord, I lift this reader up to You. Lord God, I pray that You will put Your hand on my friend here and be with them. Father, I pray that this beloved reader will open their hearts and come to know You truly as their All-Knowing God. I pray that You will bless them and keep them.
In Christ Jesus' name I pray,
Amen

God Is Faithful

Someone once asked me years ago, "What has God promised you?" At the time I had no idea. I was going through some major life difficulties. I knew there were general promises that God had made to all believers in Christ. But promised to me personally? I didn't know.

> "So know that the LORD your God is God, the faithful God. He will keep his agreement of love for a thousand lifetimes for people who love Him and obey His commands."
> ~Deut. 7:9~

"The LORD says, 'You are My witnesses and the servant I chose. I chose you so you would know and believe Me, so you would understand that I am the true God. There was no God before Me, and there will be no God after Me. I Myself am the LORD; I am the only Savior. I Myself have spoken to you, saved you, and told you these things. It was not some foreign god among you. You are My witnesses, and I am God,' says the LORD" (Isa. 43:10–12).

I do now. I know personal promises He has made in my life and for my life. If I were standing in court, I could very much put one hand on the Bible and raise the other and declare, *"As heaven and earth is my witness, I am a witness and can testify openly and honestly that God, my God, is faithful. That what God says He will do, He does."*

Shortly after I turned 37 was the first time I ever had a "word of God" really just light up in me in way I could say God heard me, answered me from His own Word, and gave me a promise I could hold to, and this came from Revelations 21:5, **"The One who was sitting on the throne said, 'Look! I am making everything new!' Then He said, 'Write this, because these words are true and can be trusted.'"**

It was during a really turbulent time in my life. You see, I have always believed there was a God and even owned a Bible. But it wasn't until my early 30s that I started studying and reading the Bible for myself, instead of just reading a verse here and there and being satisfied with someone else's thoughts and whatever lesson they wanted to share. My growing up years with God were simple. He was someone to be feared (not simply a respectful kind of fear) and if you did this, this, or this, or even if you DIDN'T do that, that, or that, you were going to hell. And since I had a whole lot of issues in my life, I had written myself off as a lost cause.

But then I started praying, and breathing without constantly feeling as if there was a hand around my throat choking me, started becoming a big thing for me. One day while I was driving to work, I literally looked in the mirror to try to see the hand choking me that felt so real. In the mirror, I didn't see it, but I kept putting my hand up to where I was sure it was at. So that day I pulled over to sit on a bench under a tree and I started praying. That was the beginning of God "reclaiming" me.

Fast forward to a few years later (to when I turned 37) after having been seriously studying the Bible and building a relationship with God, I experienced something I hadn't had before. It was on a Saturday in July and my family was gone for the weekend so I spent the whole day in just an amazing daze. "It was really weird," is the only way I could have described it back then. I didn't turn on the

> God Is Faithful

radio or the television as I didn't want anything to disrupt the incredible, peaceful silence I was experiencing. And it wasn't because everyone was gone; the peace was inside of me. I kept walking around my backyard with my hands slightly in front of me, almost tiptoeing around because it was just so peaceful. And then, in the softest of tones that I would have missed had there been any distractions I heard, "Life as you know it is going to change. Nothing will be the same. I am going to change everything." Over and over again this just kept going through me.

Over the next few days I found myself getting really excited; I couldn't wait. If God was going to do something, I was totally okay with it. But nothing changed. Well, a few little things here and there, but nothing like I had expected based on my experience on that Saturday.

Then in September, again on a Saturday, I was having a really bad day emotionally and spiritually. So I sat down and wrote God a letter. In it, I asked Him if He was really going to change EVERYTHING, regarding what I had felt He had spoken to my heart those weeks ago, did He really mean EVERYTHING? I went on to write down the list from my mind of what constituted "everything" and then I repeated, "God, are You really going to change EVERYTHING?" I underlined it so many times that I almost tore the paper, after which I put my letter away. About an hour later I was reading a book and the author had listed at the end of the chapter some verses to look up. One of them was Revelation 21:5. Now, the book I was reading had nothing to do with what I had been going through or anything I had written in my letter. It was just something that a friend of mine had given me and so I had been slowly reading it.

So that afternoon I picked it up and finished reading where I had left off. I was familiar with the other three or four verses that the author had mentioned, but I will be honest with you, I wasn't too familiar with the book of Revelation at all. So out of curiosity I got my Bible out and looked it up, and as you might be guessing by now, I about fell over! There it was, what I had just been asking God about earlier. Rev. 21:5 says, **"The One who was sitting on the throne said, 'Look! I am making everything new!' Then He said, 'Write this, because these words are true and can be trusted.'"**

As I write this chapter today, it has been over three years since that afternoon's revelation and I can say, "*Yes*, all of the things I wrote and prayed about that Saturday afternoon, I can see are finally coming to pass." However, I have to tell you, it has taken every bit of these past three years. I will also admit that sometimes I fell down in hoping I would ever see fruit from what I had believed God to promise me that Saturday. But looking back I can now see I had to be prepared for what God had planned for me.

Now I can understand how I was slowly but surely being forged. I have developed a very strong appreciation for how a small amount of water over a long period of time can create a huge canyon. What I have come to learn is that sometimes God wants to do a lot of prep work before He will bring something to pass. I noticed that every time I started to get discouraged, the verses from Joshua 1 would come to me: "Be strong and brave. Haven't I commanded you to not be discouraged?" And, *every time* I fell down in my hopes of change, God lifted me back up with: **"It is not yet time for the message to come true, but that time is coming soon; the message will come true. It may seem like a long time, but be patient and wait for it, because it will surely come; it will not be delayed"** (Hab. 2:3).

> **God Is Faithful**

However, I can also testify that during the time I now refer to as my "plowing time," God was faithful in SO MANY unexpected ways. He faithfully took care of me and my family. He provided for and protected us in so many different ways. God healed us, taught us, developed us, and changed all of us personally from the inside out. And over and over again, God has shown each of us how He loves us.

Isaiah 46:9–10 is a verse that God has repeated to me many times in the past three years: **"Remember what happened long ago. Remember that I am God, and there is no other God. I am God, and there is no one like Me. From the beginning I told you what would happen in the end. A long time ago I told you things that have not yet happened. When I plan something, it happens. What I want to do, I will do."** And, true to His Word, I am learning firsthand that *God is faithful.*

Here are the words from Hebrews 10:35–36: **"So do not lose the courage you had in the past which has a great reward. You must hold on, so you can do what God wants and receive what He has promised."** This verse is also what helped prompt me to finish this book. You see, two years before even thinking about starting this book again, I kept feeling a tug at my heart to, "Write down what I tell you." So I did. In my notebook, I began jotting down Scriptures that kept being repeated and seemed to really be speaking to me. I simply wrote verses down so often it became a habit. Plus, it was easier to meditate on them and remember what I was learning.

Then one afternoon, a friend of mine texted me that she had bought a new journal over the weekend, and it reminded her of me. So I texted her back asking why and she replied that on the cover it quoted, **"Write in a book all the words I have spoken to you"** (Jer. 30:2).

What my friend had no way of knowing was how profound her message to me would be. You see, what she didn't know was that earlier that morning I had been trying to get over a really bad headache. I hadn't been feeling well and so I decided to soak in the tub. While relaxing in the tub, I was also silently praying and trying to be still and listen, when this exact verse came to mind (very quietly), and then a short time later to my heart, a little more firmly. It was so softly spoken in me that had I been doing anything else other than lying there quietly, I would have missed it. I made a mental note to go look up the words, because I couldn't remember the exact address of the verse. I knew it was in Jeremiah, just not specifically where at. What was totally awesome for me was that I didn't have to go do a word search to find the verse being played in my heart that morning, because God delivered it right to me! I guess by now you have figured out I have started doing a lot more than just writing down Scriptures in a notebook! I want to remind you that even babies start out just living on milk. Amazingly, now I thank God for my headache that morning.

Core Study Verse Nehemiah 9:8:
"You found him faithful to you, so you made an agreement with him to give his descendants the land of the Canaanites, Hittites, Amorites, Perizzites, Jebusites, and Girgashites. You have kept your promise, because you do what is right."

What this is referring to is that Abraham believed what God had told him and was faithful in believing God would keep His promise. So, God did just that. He kept the promise He made to Abraham. Not only that, but later when we reach the end of our core study verses, you will see the Israelite's deliverance. God was faithful to

> **God Is Faithful**

them and took them into the very land He had promised 400 years earlier; He pushed out the enemy and gave victory to His people.

Granted, it took several years, okay, *many years*! But God kept His promise. Abraham dared to believe something he felt sure God had told him. And that's what I did, I finally dared to believe something I really and truly felt in my heart God had promised me. I believed He had answered me that Saturday afternoon.

At one point, when something would happen that I just couldn't pass off as being coincidental, and in my heart I believed had to be a "God thing," I started marking the Scriptures in my Bible with an orange tab. Over time when despair would hit me, I would start sinking into asking, "Did God really say...?" I would open my Bible, look at where I had placed those orange tabs, and remind myself that Jesus died on the cross. That in itself proves God is faithful. I love Luke 1:68–75:

> **"Let us praise the LORD, the God of Israel, because He has come to help His people and has given them freedom. He has given us a powerful Savior from the family of God's servant David. He said that He would do this through His holy prophets who lived long ago; He promised He would save us from our enemies and from the power of all those who hate us. He said He would give mercy to our ancestors and that He would remember His holy promise. God promised Abraham, our father, that He would save us from the power of our enemies so we could serve Him without fear, being holy and good before God as long as we live."**

Part 2: Believing God Is

You will hear me say many times in this book that God does not change. So the same faithful God before will be the same faithful God today. The problem is: sometimes you have to **BELIEVE** what you believe! Otherwise, you can do a whole lot of "believing" but actually receive very little. It reminds me of Proverbs 14:23, **"Those who work hard make a profit, but those who only talk will be poor."** You can do a whole lot of talking, but just talking isn't going to get the work done. Sometimes you have to walk the walk and show God you really *do believe* what you believe He has told you. And from my own experiences, I can tell you, in the end, *at the right time that God has set*, He Himself will show that He is faithful. I am here to tell you, God has indeed changed **EVERYTHING**! My whole life as I knew it has changed. God has been faithful to His promise. But let me tell you something He changed what I didn't expect—**ME**! He didn't just change my life; He changed *ME* inside and out. He changed the way I thought about things, some things I thought were so important, now I realize are not. He has given me new perspective in my thinking, and God has given me a new heart. In Ezekiel 36:24–27 it says,

> **"I will take you from the nations and gather you out of all the lands and bring you back into your own land. Then I will sprinkle clean water on you, and you will be clean. I will cleanse you from all your uncleanness and your idols. Also, I will teach you to respect Me completely, and I will put a new way of thinking inside you. I will take out the stubborn hearts of stone from your bodies, and I will give you obedient hearts of flesh. I will put My Spirit inside you and help live by My rules and carefully obey My laws."**

> **God Is Faithful**

I can tell you from my own experience, God really does do this. He has done this for me. In some versions it says, *"...I will give you a new heart and a new spirit in you..."* And, I am so thankful for the changes He made in me. I have also learned that it is *inside yourself* where God will start fulfilling His promise. But again, let me be a firsthand witness to you—GOD IS FAITHFUL and He has kept every promise I believe He gave to me that day when I wrote my letter to Him and He answered, *"...Write it down, because these words are true and can be trusted..."* My friend, I simply decided to take God at His word, and He did not let me down. He won't let you down, either.

**"There is a time for everything,
and everything on earth has its special season."**
(Ecc. 3:1)

In closing of God Is Faithful,

♥ PRAYING IN FAITH

Father God, we praise You. Lord God, You truly are a good and faithful God. I pray that this reader will come to know and see that. God, thank You for the testimony that You have given me that I can share with this reader. Father God, I pray that You will do the same for them in their lives, too. I pray that they will come to experience You and see Your faithfulness in their lives. I pray that they also will be able to stand up and claim as a witness for You to those around them that You are a faithful God.
In Christ Jesus' name I pray,
Amen.

> "Lord,
> you have been our home since the beginning. Before the mountains were born and before you created the earth and the world, you are God. You have always been, and you will always be."
> ~Ps. 90:1-2~

Section Break 1

Dear friend, so far we have seen how God is all-powerful, all-knowing, and faithful. It is my sincere hope you are taking the time to meditate on these names of God that He gives us. I pray as you have been reading along with me that you also can look and see how God manifests Himself as *God Is* in your life as well.

I truly hope that you are taking the time to look the verses up we are discussing for yourselves. It is amazing how God draws us to Himself when we take time to sit in quietness with just Him and our Bibles. It is important to look up Scriptures because the verses I have been compelled to share with you may or may not be the exact verses God is trying to lead you to. For example, a few days ago I was sitting in my car with my youngest son. We decided we needed some private time for just him and me to pray and sing songs—to have our own private worship time—and while he was praying he said some very powerful words!

He told Satan to stay away from him and his brothers! He also told Satan to not only get behind him, but to get off his street! And then he went further to say, "Get out of my town!" He also declared he had a right as a believer in Christ to command Satan to get behind him and some of his friends he has been concerned over. My son declared, "Jesus said, anything I ask in His name will be done, so LEAVE!" I have to tell you that I sat there stunned because I had no idea this was what his prayer of faith was going to be. But I said, "Amen!" After his prayer we sat and sang and then he asked me, "Why do we sing when we worship?" And then before I could really explain, he went into a brief discussion and asked, "Did David really chop the giant's head off?" Let me remind you that he is ten years old, so this is how our conversations sometimes go. We talked for a little bit, and I tried to answer him in a way I felt he could understand, and then we went inside.

Now, the reason I bring all this up to you, is because the next day I was enjoying my own quiet time when the first thing I did was check to see what my daily verse was. It was Psalm 104:33, **"I will sing to the LORD all my life; I will sing praises to my God as long as I live."** I smiled over it and thought, "Oh, I will have to show my son that!" Then, when opening to the devotional I like to read, I saw it quoted Matthew 16:16, so even though I knew what it said, I still looked it up. Just a few short verses down was Matt. 16:23, **"Then Jesus said to Peter, 'Go away from me, Satan!'"** And then the last devotional I went to (I do three) was about God delivering us from our enemies and one of the verses it quoted was First Sam. 17:45, **"Today the Lord will hand you over to me, and I'll kill you and cut off your head."**

I laughed and gave up any thought about having quiet time of my own that morning, and called my son in to join me. First, I showed him the verse for the day about singing, and he thought that was pretty cool, but then I showed him the first devotional I had and asked him to look it up for me. He did, but he wasn't really interested so I told him to read a little bit further. Boy, his eyes got wide! I didn't have to point it out to him. In his excitement he said, *"Mom, that's what I said! Those were MY words last night!"* He quickly got his Bible and looked it up. Because I use the NCV, it read, "Go away from me!" This was the first phrase he said in praying but, when he looked it up in his Bible, it said, "Get behind me!" which was how he phrased it the second time during his prayer.

My friend, he was amazed because, between our two Bibles, both of the ways he prayed were right there, word for word. After a bit, I encouraged him to look at my last devotional. I had to really prompt him because he was happy to just stay there. But when I got him to look at what I had been reading he got really quiet and, without hesitation, looked First Samuel 17 up in his Bible. And there it was, the whole story, including "cutting off the giant's head." My son was so excited he just kept saying, "Mom, He heard us. God must have been in the car with us last night listening."

Then he got really still and almost teary-eyed, because it dawned on him that our WHOLE conversation, not just part of it, was seen in Scripture the next morning. I have to tell you, it was such an incredible way to start out the morning with him. And my son really needed it. I am so thankful that God, knowing all the details of our lives and what is coming, worked in such a way when it was time that every detail of our sitting in the car worshipping and just visiting with each other was felt. However, had I not looked the original verses up, even though they had been quoted for me, I would have missed seeing something to share with my child and he would have missed seeing that God heard him and was present with us.

I have been quoting verses in this book to you from the NCV (New Century Version), but I encourage you to look them up in your favorite Bible version, and let God's Holy Spirit speak to you personally from His Word. I also hope you are writing in your own personal prayer space any thoughts and prayers between you and God.

So many people think "Well, that was God then, that's how God was to the people in the Bible," but God does not change. He has said so Himself over and over again. Even Jesus repeated this. What was written in the Bible is more than just a history lesson to us. Times may have changed, people may have changed, the kind of clothes we wear or the kind of houses we live in, even our vocations may have changed, but GOD has not changed.

So many people claim God doesn't speak to us like that anymore. My friend, it isn't that God doesn't speak anymore; it's that too many of us just don't want to listen. Some say, "That is just who God was to Abraham, Moses, and David." But, God wants the same friendship with us and the same closeness with us, or He wouldn't have sent His son to bear so much for us. Friend, if God didn't want to have a close personal friendship with us, He wouldn't have gone to such extremes to get our attention and draw us to Him.

A true heart of worship is a heart that seeks God all the time and welcomes Him into everyday life, into every situation. A true heart of worship is when we want to be close to Him for more than just an hour or two on Sundays, or when troubles and tribulations hit us. A heart that truly worships God is a heart that enjoys closeness with the Father each morning, throughout the day, and at night. A heart of worship laughs and cries with the Father. Jesus told the woman at the well, **"The time is coming when the true worshipers will worship the Father in spirit and truth, and that time is here already. You see, the Father too is actively seeking such people to worship him. God is spirit and those who worship Him must worship in spirit and truth"** (John 4:23). The kind of worship Jesus is speaking of is fellowship. Nothing can grow our relationship with God the Father like personal fellowship with Him. And that starts by closing our human eyes and opening our spiritual eyes and drawing close to our heavenly Father.

As we continue with our core study, we will look at God the Father as our *Liberator, Guardian, Guide, Counselor, and Provider.*

Core Study Verse: Nehemiah 9:9–15

"You saw our ancestors suffering in Egypt
and heard them cry out at the Rea Sea. You did
signs and miracles against the king of Egypt,
and against all his officers and all his people,
because You knew how proud they were.
You became as famous as You are today.
You divided the sea in front of our ancestors;
they walked through on dry ground.
But You threw the people chasing them into
the deep water, like a stone thrown into mighty
waters. You led our ancestors with a pillar of fire at
night. It lit the way they were supposed to go.
You came down to Mount Sinai and
spoke from heaven to our ancestors.
You gave them commands, orders, and teachings
through Your servant Moses. When they were
hungry, You gave them bread from heaven.
When they were thirsty,
You brought them water from the rock.
You told them to enter and take over the
land You had promised to give them."

♥ PRAYING IN FAITH

Father God, thank You for this time spent with You and what Your Word teaches us about You. Thank You for Your willingness to share so much of Yourself with us. We praise You, Father God. We praise Your holy name. Lord God, I pray that each day this reader will come to know You more personally and become closer to You. God, I hope and pray that You will manifest Your mightiness in their lives so that they too will know that You are truly God and that there is no other God.
In Christ Jesus' name I pray,
Amen.

> "I am the LORD your God, who brought you out of Egypt to be your God. I am your God."
> ~Num. 15:41~

God Is My Liberator

God is a merciful God, and He hears us when we are crying. He sees us when we are suffering. And He knows what hinders us from being with Him and having a relationship with Him. So when we finally reach that part in ourselves when more than anything else we just want HIM and we cry out to Him, God reaches out and liberates us from whatever "bondage" and "prisons" we are in that keep us from being who He has created us to be and what He intended. God loves us and doesn't want us to be separated from Him. He will tear down every stronghold that keeps us from being with Him. God says several times in His Word that He liberates us so He can be our God. **"I am the LORD who brought you out of Egypt to be your God..."** (Lev. 11:45).

Core Study Verse: Nehemiah 9:9
"You saw our ancestors suffering in Egypt and heard them cry out at the Red Sea."

God saw our ancestors. He was watching them as they went from prospering and being welcomed in Egypt (during Joseph's lifetime), to bondage and slavery under a new king that wasn't familiar with Joseph or what Joseph had done for the kingdom. God never forgot them. Some might ask, "Well, if God is such a good God, why did He let the people suffer for so long?"

We have to remember that God was looking at the very long-term picture. He was waiting until the family of Jacob had grown into MANY. God was waiting until one family had become a nation.

Part 2: Believing God Is

God was giving the family of Jacob enough time to grow and become a big enough nation so as to sustain years and generations later—all the way to our generation. God also has a timetable that must be played out. People need to be born at certain times in order to be in the right place at the right time for certain events to happen. With God, it is never just about one family, but families to come.

Maybe if we look at it in smaller proportions, it will help our hearts to understand. We have children, three boys to be exact, and sometimes our sons have to go without in order for us to provide better for them. Sometimes the things they are longing for have to wait. It's not that we don't want to give it to them. It's just that sometimes what we have in mind for them will be so much better for them in the long run. However, because they are children and their vision of life is on a smaller scale than ours, it makes it difficult for them to understand when we have to say "No" or "Not yet." There are also times the very thing they are asking for or wanting is exactly what we have planned for them, but the timing isn't right. From their perspective they are "suffering." I can admit, sometimes even for me it feels as if they are suffering, but as their parents, we have their best interests at heart. Therefore, there are times we wait, they have to endure, and we have to endure with them. I endure their time of "suffering and waiting" with a "heartfelt" heart. Even though I know the time is coming it still hurts me as I hurt with them.

It is with an extreme sigh of relief that we can read in verse 9 of Nehemiah that the right time had come and God was ready to liberate His people. I will have you know, HE WAS NOT KIDDING AROUND! There was to be retribution to the king of Egypt for his treatment of the Israelites. God wasn't sending Moses into Egypt to politely knock on the door and kindly ask for God's people to come out. No, God was sending Moses in with a message to the uppity king and the Egyptians, and with it was coming an introduction of the mighty hand of God. Under no uncertain terms was God mess-

God Is My Liberator

ing around. He had stood by for a very long time waiting until His timing was right, but at no time did He miss what His people were going through. And, when it was time, He didn't just suggest Moses should go get them, nor did He ask Moses if he would mind going on this errand for Him. No, God COMMANDED! Exodus 6:13 says: **"But the LORD spoke to Moses and Aaron and gave them orders about the Israelites and the king of Egypt. He commanded them to lead the Israelites out of Egypt."** My friend, God feels the same way about you.

Let's continue reading our core study verse:
Nehemiah 9:9-10
"...And heard them cry out at the Red Sea.
You did signs and miracles against the king of Egypt,
and against all his officers and all his people,
because You knew how proud they were."

God didn't just stop at the gates. He didn't just open the doors and say, "Here you go." He took them out of Egypt and when they got to where they couldn't go any further, God rolled up His sleeves and said, "Here, watch me."

Moses raised his staff over the Red Sea. It's easy now to look at Moses and think, *"Wow, look at what he did!"* Friend, keep in mind that at no time did God *need* Moses to raise his staff; it wasn't by Moses' strength, it was all God. If Moses hadn't been there, the waters still would have parted because His people needed a path. But the lesson for us to learn and remember is this—if we will let God, He can do amazing things THROUGH US! God can do things we could never have done on our own, but if we are willing to be a vessel for Him, watch out! Because we might just part some waters of our own!

Part 2: Believing God Is

After reading in Nehemiah, **"And heard them cry out at the Red Sea,"** I would like to compare it to another time in Scripture when it says God heard. Turn to Second Samuel 22:4–7:

> **"The waves of death came around me; the deadly rivers overwhelmed me. The ropes of death wrapped around me. The traps of death were before me. In my trouble I called to the LORD; I cried out to my God. From His temple He heard my voice; my call for help reached His ears."**

I don't know about you, but friend, when the "ropes are wrapped around me and the rivers have overwhelmed me" my cry for help is muffled and strangled! Not a vibrant "HELP!" But a strangled cry and plea, "God, please help me." Maybe your vocal cords are stronger than mine. Now, when I am as mad as a hornet, then you can bet my cry is a loud "HELP." But, when "deadly rivers have overtaken me," usually my call to God is sobbing. Of course, I am a woman, so I will admit that at those times it is in sobbing I plea for help. But I can imagine that man or woman, when you are buried so far under as to be able to describe those depths of troubles the way David did, then your cry is probably pretty pitiful to the ear. But do you know what God is doing at that moment? He's listening; He hears. And, not only does He hear, *He reacts!*

Continue reading in Second Samuel 22:8–18.

> **"The earth trembled and shook. The foundations of heaven began to shake. They trembled because the LORD was angry. Smoke came out of His nose, and burning fire came out of His mouth. Burning coals went before Him. He tore open the sky and came down with dark clouds under his feet. He rode a**

The Very Heart of Worship

God Is My Liberator

"creature with wings and flew. He raced on the wings of the wind. He made darkness his shelter, surrounded by fog and clouds. Out of the brightness of His presence came flashes of lightning. The LORD thundered from heaven; the Most High raised His voice. He shot His arrows and scattered His enemies. His bolts of lightning confused them with fear. The LORD spoke strongly. The wind blew from His nose. Then the valleys of the sea appeared, and the foundations of the earth were seen. The LORD reached down from above and took me; He pulled me from the deep water. He saved me from my powerful enemies, from those who hated me, because they were too strong for me."

How is that for a response from God? He doesn't take it lightly when one of His children needs His help. Nor does He come in ever so calmly as if to say, "Oh my, well here, let Me help." No, did you happen to read, "He tore open the sky..." I don't know about you, but when I am in way over my head, that is the kind of Liberator I need. He comes in and takes no heed of the mud I am in or how dirty His clothes are going to get! He reaches down and lifts me out and draws me to Him, filth and all. My friend, when you accept Christ and let Him into your heart, then He will do exactly the same for you.

Before we close our look at the Lord God our Liberator, I would like to share a "story," so to speak, with you. Bear with me because you will have to use your imagination to envision what I want to describe. I picture myself in that mudhole, because I have been there several times. (*No, unfortunately I did not learn the first time, which is why I want to share this vision of a story with you.*)

Anyway, in my mind I can picture my God charging in and lifting me up out of this mudhole. However, it's not so much me as a person that my mind sees, but a sheep. Well, really a lamb as it seems more fitting as a "child of God's." In my mind, I see this lamb in a massive mudhole with its head barely sticking out, crying for all he's worth, "***Help***." Then I see the Son of God, our shepherd, reaching down and lifting it up and holding it to His chest. He doesn't mind the dirt, the mud or all the muck He is now wearing on behalf of this lamb.

After cleaning His precious lamb up and feeding him, He says gently, "Now follow me." And for a while this lamb does. The lamb is so thankful to be free and clean and unburdened. He follows the shepherd for a while but then he starts looking around at the scenery and taking in how pretty it is in the meadow with this shepherd and then an interesting dragonfly comes flittering by and like a child, this lamb takes his eyes off the shepherd and starts watching this dragonfly. Then a cute little bird flies past and soon, this little lamb is off playing and frolicking around. A little while later, the lamb comes to a tall and very long brick wall. When he tries to see down the side of it, the wall just seems to go on forever.

This little lamb thinks to himself, *"I don't want to go backward!"* But since he can't see past it, he decides to try to go over it. So, he backs up a little to get a running start, leaps, and BAM, right into the brick wall! "Well, that hurt," he says to himself. He backs up a little bit farther and goes running with all his might and leaps a second time. BAM goes his head again. Lying there sprawled out with his head spinning, he thinks, *"Okay, let me try this again."* Just as he is about to go head first for the third time, he hears a soothing voice, a voice he remembers, and he looks around. There is the

> **God Is My Liberator**

shepherd! He has come looking for His lost sheep and tells His precious sheep, "Not like that, come this way. Come around, here is the path to follow."

The little lamb is very happy to see his shepherd again! So at once, he follows. With each new step the little lamb is growing and learning. But, alas, distraction comes along and again he takes his eyes off the shepherd. Before he knows it, they are separated. Now the lamb comes to a barbed wire fence. He looks at this new obstacle. It's not like the brick wall, this one he can see through so surely he can get through it! And there he goes. He gets his head through, then a left front leg and now a right front leg...so far, so good. OOPS! Now he's caught on the fence and the barbed wire is digging into his skin. He tries to pull himself out, but that only hurts more. He can't get the rest of his body past it either. Every time he tries to move, the sharp points dig in further. So he stops. And, while he is hung up on this fence, he begins to remember. He remembers the mudhole and how his shepherd rescued him. He remembers the brick wall and how the shepherd came and got him. He wonders and thinks, *"Just maybe, He can still hear me."* The little lamb puts his head back and cries, "HELP me, Lord God." And after a minute, which seems like forever to this little one, off in the distance he sees a light and it gets brighter and brighter. Then he hears it—His shepherd's voice! "Be still little one." Obediently, the lamb quits striving. Jesus kneels down next to him and untangles him from the fence. But the lamb notices this time His savior is not alone! God's Holy Spirit is protecting them from behind, and God Himself is up ahead covering them and protecting them with His mighty hand!

When Jesus frees the little lamb, He notices that His precious one is all cut up and hurt. He carefully soothes His lamb with oil and bandages the wounds, but He doesn't put the lamb down! Nope, Jesus cradles His lost one to His chest and whispers lovingly in the lamb's ear, "I am so happy to find you! I have come for you." And this time as they travel, the lamb is tucked safely in his shepherd's arms and the mighty light of God leads them ahead while God's Holy Spirit protects them from behind. They all travel together, the lamb, his shepherd and his mighty God.

> **"He takes care of His people like a shepherd. He gathers them like lambs in His arms and carries them close to Him. He gently leads the mothers of the lambs."**
> (Isa. 40:11)

In closing of God Is My Liberator,

♥ PRAYING IN FAITH

Father God, we praise You as our Liberating God. Lord, thank You for your willingness to tear open the skies on our behalf. Thank You, that You rescue us and carry us in Your arms close to You. Lord, thank You, that if need be, You will move heaven and earth to get to us. Lord, we praise You for there is no place Your arm cannot reach.

Father God, thank You for this time spent studying Your Word with my friend who is reading along with me. Lord, I pray for this friend and ask that whatever holds this reader captive, and any bondage around this reader, be removed. I pray that You will liberate this precious child of Yours from whatever strongholds hinder them from You and all that You would have for them. Lord, I ask You to go after them and set them free from any fences they may be caught upon. Thank You, Lord God, for listening and hearing our cries to You.
In Christ Jesus' name I pray,
Amen.

> "He will not let you be defeated.
> He who guards you never sleeps.
> He who guards Israel never rests or sleeps."
> ~Ps. 121:3-4~

God Is My Guardian

Dear friend, I hope you are beginning to see our God in a whole new, personal way. Before we start this new chapter, I want to let you know that it will be a little bit longer than the previous ones as I have a few personal testimonies about how God watches over us and protects us that I would like to share with you. But first, in our next core study verse we look at:

Nehemiah 9:11
"You divided the sea in front of our ancestors; they walked through on dry ground. But You threw the people chasing them into the deep water, like a stone thrown into mighty waters."

Isn't it amazing that it doesn't mention ANY of the Israelites being lost during the crossing! Just imagine that many people crossing over, but the waters remained parted until the last one made it past. However, when the enemy started to follow, God's reaction was, *"Not so fast!"*

If you back up from where Nehemiah was reading about the crossing of the Red Sea, we will see that long before this God was already guarding them. Exodus 12:40–42 says, **"The people of Israel had lived in Egypt for four hundred thirty years; on the very day the four hundred thirty years ended** *(notice there was a set time)* **the LORD'S divisions of people left Egypt. That night the LORD kept watch to bring them out of**

Egypt, and so on this same night the Israelites are to keep watch to honor the LORD from now on."

Did you see what God did? He kept watch. There were only 70 members in Jacob's family (also called Israel) starting out in Egypt, but when it came time for them to leave 430 years later they had to go out in divisions! What a huge family! And I think it's a large gathering when my brothers and our whole families get together. But notice God watched over them all night as they left the land where they had become slaves. Then watch what God did. Exod. 14:19–20 says, **"Now the angel of God that usually traveled in front of Israel's army moved from in front of the people and stood behind them. So the cloud came between the Egyptians and the Israelites. This made it dark for the Egyptians but gave light to the Israelites. So the cloud kept the two armies apart all night."**

I would like to share a few stories of God's protection I have witnessed with my own eyes. The first testimony is starting with our youngest son. When he was only five years old, we had taken the boys out motorcycle riding. Our youngest had a little "lady bug" four-wheeler. He loved that thing! He would spend the whole time riding up and down the trail that circled around this huge dirt bowl where people on motorcycles and four-wheelers would ramp up and jump. Every time my son would come by me he would give me a thumbs-up. This one particular day, there weren't a lot of people around. There were only a few men on some rather large monster four-wheelers and, of course, our other two sons on their motorcycles. All morning long, the men on the four-wheelers had been coming down off the trail and coming up to the bowl in front of us and ramping—flying over the bowl, then somewhere just before reaching the other side of this dirt bowl they would shift their handle bars toward the left, land, and ride off back up the trails.

The Very Heart of Worship

God Is My Guardian

Now keep in mind, we had been watching this all day. They would come down off the trail on the right side, circle around, jump the bowl, then go off to the left and out of sight. All day long like clockwork. Our youngest son had been watching this also and knew where to stop and watch for them. Later on that afternoon, he came down off the trail on the right side of this dirt bowl and stopped. He had just seen one of the men in front of him coming down off the trail, heading for the bowl's dirt ramp. He waited at the edge of the trail so as not to cut in front or get in the way of the rider. The only problem was that THIS TIME the rider didn't pivot toward the left, like they had been doing all day. THIS TIME he shifted and went to the right! He didn't see my son sitting there until he was already in the air and coming down. My youngest son watched in terror as this rider on his monster four-wheeler was coming right at him. No one could do anything except start screaming and running toward the accident coming into play.

Luckily I was not sitting there alone. Alongside the entrance to the area where we would take the boys riding was also where everyone would park their vehicles and sit while taking turns riding or resting. So there were a few people sitting by their vehicles watching the riders going back and forth. And when this rider who was ramping shifted to the right, we all saw what he couldn't. Everyone started hollering and running. By the time we got to the other side, which really wasn't that far away (though it seemed like an incredibly long time to get there), the man had landed on my son.

The way it looked coming up to them was that somehow this man must have, at the last second, seen my son and leaned off his four-wheeler to knock my son off of his. When the four-wheeler landed, he and my son went flying in one direction and the two four-wheelers went another direction.

My son's little four-wheeler went flying through the air and landed in a heap, totaled. The man's four-wheeler landed just off the side of my son's, a little banged up. But the man and my son landed in a different spot altogether! And there was not one broken bone for either of them. However, my son couldn't walk very well, so we pulled his jeans down (they weren't even ripped), and found a massive bruise with a few cuts on the underside of his left leg, behind his knee. That was it. That was the extent of the injuries. The man was fine, but he was scared to death and couldn't quit shaking or apologizing. However, my son's four-wheeler was never ridden again.

The next story I would like to share is about this same son only two years later. He was playing at a friend's house and the friend's mom, in tears, called me saying I needed to come over and get my son and take him to the doctor's office as he had been hurt. She felt horrible about him getting hurt while in her care! With my son being the youngest of three boys and me coming from a home with brothers, boys getting hurt is not new to me. But, my youngest son is the same age as her twins, her only children, so this was new for her. I didn't know who I felt worse for, her or my son, until I got there and was able to see what had happened.

When I got there, my son was lying on the couch in tears waiting for me. It looked as if he had broken his collarbone. We took him to the doctor, and yes, it was a broken collarbone. The doctor also checked him out for any other injuries, before giving him a sling and some pain medication. Then the doctor scheduled a follow-up visit and sent us home. But, my story doesn't end there.

On the way home, I stopped back by my friend's house to pick up my son's things and to let her sons know that everything was okay. Now I really wish I had just stopped at that. But I didn't. Her little boys wanted to take me outside to show me where and how the accident occurred. I walked out back to the fort they have near the

God Is My Guardian

back of the yard, which was sitting pretty close to the fence. Apparently, the three of them decided to eat lunch in the fort, so while my friend was inside getting lunch for them the boys were up in the fort moving some little chairs around.

Unfortunately, they put one chair too close to the opening in the back. When my son sat down in it, the chair tipped over—falling through the opening to the "fireman's pole" and landing in the dirt below with my son in it, head down. One of the twins said, "Here, let me show you, it fell like this…" Seeing the foot and a half of space that my son landed in and then hearing the thud of the chair hitting the ground was all my heart could take, making me sick to my stomach. I don't know how my son managed to fall in such a small amount of space, and land on his head with this chair on top of him, and only break his collarbone. It was a wonder he hadn't broken his neck.

I give complete thanksgiving and glory to God. The results of these incidents could only have been by God's divine protection. I truly believe God was watching over my son and protecting him. Did he get hurt? Yes, but could it have been so much worse? Yes. Praise to God that it wasn't.

The last story I would like to share in witness to God's guardianship is about my middle son. Sorry, but it is another wrestling story. He was at a tournament and was wrestling for third place. The kid he was against was good and neither one could get the other down, so it was just back and forth with each of them getting points. At the start of the third period, my son was on top of the opponent and was trying to get him down. They went off the mat, and on to the gym floor out-of-bounds. The referee blew his whistle, stopping them so they could reposition. Just as my son let go and was sitting up, the boy he was wrestling reached up and, in a very cheap move, grabbed my son's head, slamming it on the gym floor. It totally took my son by surprise. Even from where I was sitting in the stands—with a gym full of people and several other matches going on at the same time—I heard the thud of my son's head hitting the ground.

The referee pulled the other kid off my son, who was now lying on the ground. The coaches went running over to him. After helping my son up and seeing his dazed look, the head coach looked up into the stands and waved for me to come down. By the time I was able to get over to where the mats were, I could see the back of my son standing in front of three of his coaches. One of the coaches had his hand on my son's face, one of the other coaches had his hand on my son's shoulder, and both were looking at his head and talking to him. So there I stood, waiting. The next thing I know, I saw the coaches kind of grin, tell my son "Okay," and put their arms down and back up. I'm thinking, *"Okay, what?"*

I watched as my son walked over to the center of the mat. The referee started to walk over, but my son held up his hand as if to say, "Stay over there and leave me alone." Then he turned his hand to the opponent who had just given him the cheap shot and waved his hand to the other boy in a gesturing motion and said, "Come on, let's go." All I could do was sit back down and hold my breath. It took less than 30 seconds. My son had the other guy down on his back, pinning him for the win.

Everyone came up and pounded my son on the shoulder, then he went over to the table and got his medal for third place, before going behind the table and sitting down to catch his breath. But didn't get back up!

For ten minutes I waited for him to come over to the stands where I was sitting, but he never did. My youngest son went looking for him and found him sitting behind the score table with his head

God Is My Guardian

between his knees. No one realized that he was hurt. You see, it isn't uncommon for some of the wrestlers to sit back behind there after their match to "settle down." My youngest son found him and then came and got me. When I got over there, he said he had a headache and he felt kind of dizzy. So I helped him up, got him an icepack and some aspirin, and we sat with him until he felt better. After a while, he was walking around and people we didn't even know kept coming up to congratulate him. He finally asked me what they were talking about. He had no memory of walking out to the center of the mat, no memory of holding his hand up to the referee to back off, and no memory of telling the other kid, "Come on, let's go." He just knew he had gone out there and finished the match and somehow won.

We talked about it and he said it must have been a "God thing!" Because when he couldn't, God must have said, "It's okay, I can." I understand now that as I was watching my son walk back out on the mat, so confident and sure of himself, that it wasn't him—or it wasn't *just* him. God walked out there with him, God defended him, and God gave him a very swift victory.

How can I be so sure in crediting this as a victory from God? Because Jesus says that all Scripture is true. God Himself said He does not change. So when we accept God into our lives, when we accept Jesus as our Lord and Savior, God steps into the ring. And when someone comes up against us, they come up against God.

God doesn't force Himself on us. He gives us a choice. He tells us over and over again that if we will listen to Him, if we will honor Him and His name, if we will follow Him, He will give us blessings and be with us and watch over us. But, in the same way that He promises good things, He promises the opposite if we turn away from him to follow false gods and worship other idols (read Deuteronomy chapters: 4, 6, 7, and 28 and also Joshua 23).

Deuteronomy 11:26 says,

> **"See, today I am letting you choose a blessing or a curse. You will be blessed if you obey the commands of the LORD your God that I am giving you today. But you will be cursed if you disobey the commands of the LORD your God."**

If you turn over to chapter 30, you will see in verse 15, **"Look, today I offer you life and success, death and destruction."** And then in verse 19, **"Today I ask heaven and earth to be witnesses. I am offering you life or death, blessings or curses. Now choose life!"**

Some people may question, "Well, if God is so good, then why..." But we have to remember, God told the Israelites in Exodus 23, **"Your enemies will become my enemies...I will fight those that come against you,"** so apparently we will have enemies, we will have other people who will come up against us. In Isaiah 43, God said, **"When you pass through the waters and walk through fire...I will be with you."** Again, apparently we will have some major tough times but God promises to be with us THROUGH THEM. That means we are going to have them, but we can rest assured we will come through them and that there will be an end. Even Jesus told His followers that in this life we will have trouble. But He also comforted them by saying, **"I have defeated the world"** (John 16:33).

Again, some people may question, "Why?" Because life on this earth is not our final destination. If life were picture perfect here,

God Is My Guardian

with no sorrow and no pain, and heaven on earth, we would never want to leave. We would never want to arrive at our final destination, which is WITH GOD. Where we are now is just a stepping stone. And in this life there are going to be valleys. But as much as the valleys hurt, it's in the valleys where we come to know God. It's in the valleys we grow closer to Him and where we see His glory as we watch Him do things we can't.

Though God might have come to my son's aid instantly in the story I just shared with you, we also have to remember that in a lot of cases God's assistance, or even defense, may be later when we are not even aware of it, or have had to wait for it. But take heart because God is a just God. Even if we do not see instant action from God, it doesn't mean He isn't going to help, or that He hasn't noticed or doesn't care.

If you read in First Samuel 17, the Israelites went through 40 days of taunting before victory was seen or even won. The reason being? The vessel through which God was going to show His victory wasn't there yet. He was at home getting ready to be sent. (Of course I am referring to the story of David and Goliath.) The whole time the enemy was tormenting the Israelites, God was working behind the scenes putting everything into place. God had a plan, and He had someone specific to carry out that plan, and God was sending him.

Sometimes what we can't see when we are being tormented, while we are in a huge battle, is that God can see it all from up on His mountain and He is working it out. When we are limited by our sight we have to remember that from His vantage point God can see it all and is working things out and putting His plans into action in ways we can't see from where we are at.

So we have a decision to make; we are given a choice. What side do we want to be on? We have to decide, who's our God? As for me, I will take the mighty God of Israel. I may not always understand what He is doing or what is happening. But I will toss my hat into God's ring every time. The words from Joshua 24:15 come to mind:

> **"But if you don't want to serve the LORD you must choose for yourselves today whom you will serve. You may serve the gods that your ancestors worshiped when they lived on the other side of the Euphrates River, or you may serve the gods of the Amorites who lived in this land. As for me and my family, we will serve the LORD."**

Dear friend, God really is a mighty God. Let's you and I take Him at His Word. If He is for us, then who can be against us? When you're going through horrible storms, take heart and know that you are not alone. The same strong voice that commanded the stormy waters to be quiet so long ago (Mark 4:39), can and will do the same for you. The same God who **"drove back the sea with a strong east wind, making the sea become dry ground"** (Exod. 14:21), will do the same for you.

I would like to leave you with some key memory verses. I will just list them instead of quoting them for you, so that you can look them up and see how they read in your favorite Bible version. The next time your back is to the wall or you are coming up against opposition, hang on to God's Word and ask Him for protection and guardianship.

(Ps. 59:16–17)   (Joel 3:16)
(Ps. 140:6)   (Ps. 62:1)   (Heb. 13:8)

In closing of God Is My Guardian,

♥ <u>**PRAYING IN FAITH**</u>

Father God, thank You for all the times You have watched over us, even at times when we were unaware of it. Lord God, we praise You for Your protection during our battles.

Lord, thank You for Your promise that when we come to rough waters, trials, and tribulations, we are not alone, that You are with us. Thank You, that You go before us and with us each step of the way. Lord God, again we thank You for this time spent with You in Your Word. Lord, thank You for this reader, please be with them and watch over them. Lord, I ask You to protect them in whatever they may be going through.
In Christ Jesus' name I pray,
Amen.

> "Then I will lead the blind along a way they never knew;
> I will guide them along paths they have not known.
> I will make the darkness become light for them, and the rough grounds smooth.
> These are the things I will do;
> I will not leave my people."
> ~Isa. 42:16~

God Is My Guide

In the next core study of Nehemiah 9, we see that God's protection didn't stop at the parting of the Red Sea. He protected them day and night and gave them direction. He was their compass and showed them which way to go. He didn't take them out of Egypt, part the seas for them, and then tell them to simply cross the desert and make their own way over to the Jordan River, where He would meet them to give them further instructions. Nope, God went with them day and night and guided them every step of the way. He didn't leave them. And guess what? He still does the same today!

<u>Core Study Verse: Nehemiah 9:12</u>
**"You led our ancestors with a pillar of cloud
by day and with a pillar of fire at night.
It lit the way they were supposed to go."**

I would like to stop here for a moment and share with you a bit of my own "crossing." Almost a year prior to the time I am writing this, I was sitting in my car at a church parking lot, not too far from the house, looking in the rearview mirror contemplating where to go. The place I was at is where I like to go periodically when I need quiet time to think but isn't as far away from the house as my special prayer place is.

Part 2: Believing God Is

There is more to this story I will share with you later in a different chapter, but for now I will summarize the events so that I can focus on what I consider to be part of God's divine direction.

It was a Friday morning and I hadn't been outright terminated, but I hadn't actually quit my job either. However, I had just experienced an eruption that had been extremely unexpected and a little bit shocking. After the dust had settled, I realized that God was saying, "I have plans for you and if you won't move on your own, I will move you." When I think back, I am reminded that even the Israelites didn't want to leave Egypt at first. But one way or the other, God had plans for them, and leaving is what they were going to do! So when it came time for me to go on to what God's purpose for me was, He made sure that I moved!

So there I was on this Friday morning. I had already gone to a place where I had known for a while they'd needed a manager, but the week prior they had found someone. I have to tell you that instead of being upset or worried, I was at peace. I didn't know where I was going or what I was going to do but at that moment I was not surprised the position had been filled nor was I overly concerned about my next move, which was why I was sitting in my parking space. I was somewhere between praying and just talking to God. Every so often I would look in the rearview mirror at the traffic driving past on the main street behind me. Verses kept coming to mind: *"Seek first the kingdom of God..." "Be still and know that I am God..." "For I know the plans I have for you..." "Don't go away searching, stay where you are..."*

I remember sitting there letting this concordance of verses filter through my mind. Again, I caught myself looking in my review mirror but after remembering Lot's wife looking back and becoming a pillar of salt, I stopped. After a while, I drove down to a spot at the river that is very important to me and went to my favorite place to pray. And pray I did! I didn't so much pray for help as I did surren-

The Very Heart of Worship

God Is My Guide

der to God. Then I went home to spend time with my family. My thoughts were that it was a Friday and nothing could really be done at the end of the week so I would wait until Monday to get a fresh start. Dear friend, I never had to. And this is the part of the story that I really want to discuss with you.

That evening it was brought up by a friend that I should go back into business for myself—that I should start doing private bookkeeping for small businesses. I was totally against it, thinking there was no way, we didn't have the finances, the timing wasn't right ... the list went on and on. Then an interesting thing happened; my friend asked me what I would call it. Out of my mouth came "Cypress." When I was asked why, and what was a cypress, I found myself looking around the room trying to see what in the world would have brought that word to and out of my mouth.

I had a fleeting image in my mind of the huge tree I was sitting under earlier while I was praying, but as I said, it was fleeting so I didn't think much more of it. I went on to explain that down South, where I am from, a cypress is a huge tree. As we were talking, the thought of "Cypress Bookkeeping" became more of a possibility. Before going to bed that night I got on my knees and prayed, telling God I didn't know what He was up to or what He was doing, but I trusted Him. If this was something I should consider doing then I was willing, but He was going to have to bring it to pass.

The next morning I got up and made coffee for everyone, then sat down with a devotional I had been reading. It was a nice devotional, though I will admit that now I can't quite remember what it was about, but it referred to a passage in Isaiah 55. Now, I am no Bible scholar, but I am somewhat familiar with Isaiah 55; however, for the life of me I couldn't think what part of Isaiah 55 the writer of the devotional would be pulling from in reference to his topic. So, I got my Bible to look it up. Yes, Isaiah 55 was what I thought it was, but I kept on reading and in the last two verses of Isaiah 55 this is what I read:

> **"So you will go out with joy and be led out in peace. The mountains and hills will burst into song before you, and all the trees in the field will clap their hands. Large cypress trees will grow where thorn bushes were. These things will be a reminder of the LORD's promise, and this reminder will never be destroyed."**

I have to tell you, I sat there dumbfounded! I read it and reread it! There it was: "cypress trees." Now I am thinking and wondering, what are the odds of that? I was already convinced that this was a "God thing." There was nothing the night before to have brought the thought of "cypress trees" to my mind and out of my mouth, so in my heart I was already reeling from this, but just to appease the skeptic in me, I did a word search. Keep in mind there are over 31,000 verses in the Bible. I chose the four most common Bible versions plus my own preferred version. I figured five times 31,000 verses is 155,000, so how many times would a word search of "cypress trees" produce results? *Seven times.* Out of over 155,000 Bible verses from these five Bibles, the phrase "cypress trees" only came up in seven verses. When I looked to see what terms were used instead, I found several places in the different versions said "large pine trees" instead of cypress.

Not only did God give me the name, but He did it in such a way that "in my language" I saw and understood it. If I had just read the phrase "large pine trees" you probably wouldn't be reading this now, because I would not have thought anything else about it.

> **God Is My Guide**

But you have to remember that when God is working in us, or talking to us, He will do it in a way or in a "language" we can understand. When God is giving us directions, He isn't going to speak Spanish to you if all you speak and understand is English.

If it had been one of my sons reading their Bible that morning, Isaiah 55:13 says, "large pine trees." They would never have thought anything else about it. But, because I had been praying for direction and guidance and asking God ("What do you want me to do?"), when He gave me direction, He made sure it would come up and be confirmed to me in a way that I would see it and understand that He had spoken. I often think of the sign above the cross when Jesus was crucified and how the same phrase was written several times in different languages so everyone there would be able to read and understand it.

However, my story of God's divine direction doesn't stop there. After reading these verses and doing a word search, my mind started racing. By that afternoon, I had found a completely furnished office, and quite a bit of temp work along with it. By Monday, I was opening a checking account and was bonded. Two weeks to the day that I sat in the parking lot, I was sitting in my new office working. And life was amazingly good. For all of three and a half months!

For three and a half months, temp work kept coming; I was staying really busy and I was convinced God had put me in that office, doing what I was doing. But I could never get full-time assignments. It was just one temporary assignment after another. Then it started slowing down until several months later I came to a complete standstill! I couldn't go this way, I couldn't go that way, and I sure didn't want to go backward, but there was no going forward either. In fact every time I would start to pray, the term "standstill" was what I kept coming back to. I kept praying and asking God for clarity. I knew He had led me to it—I knew He had put me there—but I didn't understand why so I kept asking Him what the "standstill" I had come to was all about.

Then over and over again, everywhere I turned, every time I read anything, including sermons and devotionals, everything kept coming back to "health" and "healing." I started reading about healing and health. Also Jeremiah 33 started becoming a major Scripture reference. Someone was always quoting something from Jeremiah 33, so one morning I decided to slowly, and with openness, read Jeremiah 33. What startled me was verse 6: **"But then I will bring health and healing to the people there."**

One evening I was listening to a sermon podcast while I was working on some things. I was listening but not real intently. The sermon was about Paul's imprisonment in his own home for two years. The pastor was talking about how active Paul had been and that his primary objective before this imprisonment had been starting and planting new churches, so it must have been quite something for Paul when God had brought him to this standstill in his life.

As you can guess, this got my attention very quickly! Now I was listening very intently. In fact I rewound it just to hear those words over again! Yes, the pastor really said Paul had come to a standstill in his life! God had brought him to a point where he couldn't just keep going and going. But what others might have viewed, and had even intended, as an imprisonment, God was using for good. It gave Paul much needed time for rest and to physically heal. It also gave Paul time to write four of our New Testament books that may not have been written had Paul not had the downtime his imprisonment had given him.

> **God Is My Guide**

Immediately, I was brought to conviction! I knew what my standstill and downtime was about. A few years earlier I had started the rough drafts to this book you are holding and one other. But for many reasons I was forced to put them down, then aside, and after awhile completely out of mind!

I spent several days in prayer about this and the whole "cypress" thing. I asked for wisdom, understanding and most of all clarity! It started becoming clear. God had brought to me and given me the name "Cypress" and I added bookkeeping to it and ran with it! God gave me an office, He gave me divine guidance, and even gave me a name, but then I went racing with it. I realized then that God was trying to do something totally NEW in my life, but I was trying to turn it into something I was familiar with. I was trying to take the leading and direction God was giving me and turn it into something I could do!

I quickly began to have a new appreciation for Joshua 3:1–5: **"Early the next morning Joshua and all the Israelites left Acacia. They traveled to the Jordan River and camped there before crossing it. After three days the officers went through the camp and gave orders to the people; When you see the priests and Levites carrying the Ark of the Agreement with the LORD your God, leave where you are and follow it. That way you will know which way to go since you have never been here before. But do not follow too closely. Stay about a thousand yards behind the Ark. Then Joshua told the people 'Make yourselves holy, because tomorrow the LORD will do amazing things among you.'"**

Now to bring us back to our study of God as our Guide. There are several lessons here I hope you are learning and grasping. Also, I hope that in sharing my story, it will help you to have confidence in the fact that (1) God does give us divine guidance, and (2) when God is ready, He will take you someplace completely new! But I also hope that in sharing my story with you, you will learn from my mistake in following too closely so you don't wind up in front of God, and then detouring from what it is He is trying to do.

Just like the Israelites, I had never been this way before so I needed to focus on God. Yet Joshua told the people: don't get too far away from the ark, but don't get too close either. I understand both reasons now. I guess hindsight really is 20/20. If we don't stay focused on God and we get too far behind, we run the risk of getting distracted and losing our way completely. But, on the other hand, if we follow too closely we run the risk of running out ahead of Him trying to do it our way and then we realize we've missed a step or even a turn!

If you will look back at our core verse of Nehemiah 9:12, God led them by day and by night. He led them each step of the way, every day. He stayed with them and continued to make a path for them, long after the waters had parted and then closed back. My friend, know that He has done this for me over and over again, and He will do the same for you if you will let Him. He is willing and more than able to lead you through any "crossings," whether it is water or desert you have to go through. Just don't be afraid if you find He is taking you someplace completely new and unfamiliar to you. Trust me, or better yet, trust God. He knows the way and will lead you on the right path if you will focus on Him and ask for His guidance.

In closing of God Is My Guide

♥ PRAYING IN FAITH

Father God, thank You for the experiences You have given me that I may share with this reader and others. Lord, I pray that as my friend here comes to know You more, that they also will have a journey to repeat as testimony for You. Thank You for Your promise that if we will stay focused with our eyes to You, that You will lead us and make our paths straight and light the darkness so that we may follow You.

Once again, Lord, thank You for this time in Your Word. I also continue to pray for this dear reader, and ask that You will lead them and guide them on the path You have for them. I ask You, Lord, to shed Your light on them so that they may see what steps to take.
In Christ Jesus' name I pray,
Amen.

> "Then David asked the LORD, 'Should I chase the people who took our families? Will I catch them?' The LORD answered, 'Chase them. You will catch them, and you will succeed in saving your families.'"
> ~1 Sam. 30:8-9~

God Is My Counselor

Welcome back. Let's get right to our core study verse.

<u>Nehemiah 9:13-14</u>:
"You came down to Mount Sinai and spoke from heaven to our ancestors. You gave them fair rules and true teachings, good orders and commands. You told them about Your holy Sabbath and gave them commands, orders and teachings through Your servant Moses."

Dear friend, one of the things that is so awesome about God is that at no time does He expect us to go it alone. This is the same God who knitted us together. This is the same God who created the universe. Glory to His Name Most High!

When you think about the complexity of how our bodies are made up or look at nature and the incredible structure of our planet, I have to tell you, God is a God of details! So, in knowing this about our God, we have to know He has complete knowledge and wisdom about what's up ahead. He isn't about to take us out into the wilderness and just drop us off and expect us to fend for ourselves. We, as New Testament believers, (and by that I mean that we are on this side of the cross), get to go up and ask for counsel from the Almighty God! At any given time we are welcome to drop to our knees and ask God, "Where do I go from here? What do I do now?"

Part 2: Believing God Is

Before the cross, God's people were still able to seek God's counsel; however, they did it through their leaders or the high priest. But whether we are speaking about the people on that side of the cross or our generation now after Christ's crucifixion, we still are referring to a God who wants to be the God of His people. And that, my friend, means that when we have questions, when we have problems, when we have a need for direction or for someone bigger than ourselves; we have a God who is concerned. We have a God who loves His people, a God who is willing to give counsel and put us on course, shed light for us, move mountains for us, and go before us and show us the way.

It is important to be in a walk with God daily, to be in a habit of regular prayer and relationship with God at all times. It is equally important to look to Him for guidance before making an assumption. What God had us do at one point is not necessarily what He would have us to do the next time, though the situation may look similar. Just because something comes our way that looks like something we have dealt with before does not mean that what worked before will work now. Don't forget, at one time God had Moses hit a rock to provide water for His people, but then later, on a separate occasion, God had Moses speak to a rock. However, Moses didn't obey, and it cost him entrance into the Promised Land.

Another biblical reference I would like you to look at is First Chronicles 14, starting in verse 8. The Philistines had heard that David had been made king so they came up to attack David. But, look at what David did. He asked God, "Is this what I should do?" And God, because He was asked, answered him.

> **"David asked God, 'Should I go and attack the Philistines? Will you hand them over to me?'**

The Very Heart of Worship

God Is My Counselor

The LORD answered him, 'Go, I will hand them over to you'" (vs. 10).

David did indeed have victory. But later the Philistines attacked a second time. Again we read that David asked counsel of the LORD, and it is a good thing he did because this time God had different instructions for David. Look at verses 14–15:

> **"David prayed to God again, and God answered him, saying, 'Don't attack the Philistines from the front. Instead, go around them and attack them in front of the balsam trees. When you hear the sound of marching in the tops of the balsam trees, then attack. I, God, will have gone out before you to defeat the Philistine army.'"**

Twice God gave David victory over the enemy, but in different ways. Imagine what might have happened if David had not asked. Before this incident, David didn't ask God for direction on how something was to be done, and it cost a man his life. If you back up to chapter 13 in First Chronicles, David, along with the Israelites, decided it was a good idea to bring the Ark of the LORD back to Jerusalem. This seemed like an easy enough venture so they raced on ahead to accomplish it. But what David forgot, or maybe didn't realize, was that God had a very specific way for the Ark to be carried. Only Levites were to transport it. And since David failed to inquire of the LORD first, he missed one key bit of information that would have made a huge difference. Later on in chapter 15:11–13 David admits his failure to ask God how to carry the Ark.

Having key bits of information makes a difference! A while back our oldest son had a friend spend the night and the next morning, on the way to a tournament for our other two sons, I was taking this

Part 2: Believing God Is

friend home. I have to admit it was getting close to the time I needed to be at the gym, and I was getting really aggravated with the directions I was given to take this young man home. The boys couldn't seem to give me a clear address or even a clear street name and, unfortunately, we have two bridges in the town we live in and my son got them confused. In my frustration (because I couldn't understand why this young man couldn't give better directions on how to get to his house), I turned my head to the right to ask them, "DOES ANY OF THIS LOOK FAMILIAR; AM I EVEN IN THE RIGHT PLACE?" The next thing I know, BAM! I hit a car that was turning through the intersection I was entering.

Luckily, no one was hurt. But an hour later, after the police had finished up everything, I found out my son's friend had been in town for less than three weeks. No wonder he was having such a hard time telling me how to get home! I told my son later, "That bit of information would have been extremely helpful."

Going back to our core verse in Nehemiah 9, the Israelites had just spent the past 430 years in Egypt as slaves. They weren't going to know their way through the desert, much less how to live each day, without some help. God was in no way planning to make them fend for themselves. He doesn't expect us to either, especially if He is taking us out of one place and bringing us to a new place altogether.

In the last chapter I spoke about my crossing into something new. I shudder to think of what all I would have missed if I hadn't stopped to ask God for His counsel that Friday. Or even several months later, when things weren't working out as I had planned. I could have just assumed that I had "misunderstood." In fact I had several people ask the whole Eve question, "Now did God really

God Is My Counselor

say...?" I could have, in my discouragement, decided maybe this wasn't what I was supposed to do. But I kept looking back at my journal of the "Cypress trees" and what came about over the course of the following months.

If I have learned anything, it is that God is faithful and God doesn't lie. I knew there was no way that the name "Cypress" had just somehow come from me and, by random chance, it was in the Bible verses I was to read the next day. I did not imagine the furnished office and everything that fell into place over the next few days. And let me tell you, I strongly suggest that when God is moving in your life, write it down! Journal it and pick up a few of your own Ebenezer stones to remind yourself, "That thus far, God has helped" (see First Samuel 7). You will need them. It's very easy for the enemy to rob you of your memories of God's faithfulness when you are going through struggles or unexpected battles. It's very easy for your shield of faith to become a mass of doubts when going through seasons that look like the dead of winter. But if you will journal your "God Movements," if you will write down the traces of God's hand you have experienced, then it is easier to hold on to the truth of God's handiwork in your life during seasons of limited sight.

So when I came to what seemed to be a wrong direction leading right into a dead-end, I asked God, "What is this all about?" Had I somehow misunderstood the direction He was giving me? Did I take a wrong turn? I knew that God had moved me to this point, but I didn't have clarity or understanding. Instead of throwing my hands up in the air and saying, "Oh well," I went to God and asked for counsel. I prayed for understanding.

I am so glad I did. Because what I found is that yes, God was moving me, and if I would just wait and spend some time at God's

Part 2: Believing God Is

feet I would see that He had some major plans. Not just for me, but my whole family. Sometimes we, as humans, think we constantly have to be "doing." We don't realize that at certain times the most important thing we really need to be doing is following Mary's example and sitting at Jesus' feet (see Luke 10:38–42). Most often, when God wants to do something new in our lives, He will start off first requesting we spend a season of quietness with just Him. During these seasons we need to take some time to just learn from Him and give Him a chance to come in and clean house—to let Him revamp some things in us, to restructure us, and most importantly, to heal or repair any needs in us before moving us forward.

While Mary was spending time with Jesus, her sister Martha, was busy cooking, hosting, and serving everyone. My friend, sometimes we have to realize that every once in a while we need to take a break and tell everyone they can eat sandwiches, because Jesus is in the house and we are spending time with Him!

If you don't take time to get direction from God, then it is very easy to miss a key step, and you can wind up in the wilderness all alone wondering, "Where did everybody go?" Also, spending seasons in quietness with God allows for Him to plant things in us that will grow into amazing events if we will let Him work in us. What you have to know in advance, though, is sometimes God has to go in and prepare our hearts and our minds before He can start doing any planting in us. And if you are anything like I was, sometimes you have to let Him go in and pull some weeds and plow the soil first. But my, oh my, is it ever so worth it! Glory truly is to God!

The other incredible thing about God as our counselor is that we can come before Him in complete openness, as He already knows our hearts, and we don't have to hide anything from Him. Nothing will shock Him. He welcomes us to come and just sit in His presence and talk to Him. Sometimes the best prayers are not what we are

> **God Is My Counselor**

asking of Him, but instead just visiting with Him, opening up to Him, and letting His holiness infiltrate us. Often we miss the most important part of prayer with God, and that is just spending time in fellowship while basking in His warmth.

Don't wait until you need "know-how" before going to God. Spend some time growing your relationship with Him during the calm seas so when storms do arise or challenges occur you will be ready and adept at hearing and listening to God. You will be more in tune with Him and will know with more certainty what details He is providing to you so that you can follow with sure footing.

> **"The LORD says, 'I will make you wise and show you where to go. I will guide you and watch over you'"** (Psalm 32:8).

In closing of God Is My Counselor,

♥ PRAYING IN FAITH

Father God, how good You are to us. Thank You for the counsel You so willingly give us. Thank You that at any time we can come before You and just rest in Your presence. I praise Your wonderful name, Lord God Most High. You are the creator of the heavens and the earth, yet You still bend Your ear to us to listen and give us the direction and guidance we need.

Thank You, for this time spent in Your Word and for teaching us. Father, I pray that You will continue to be with this reader follow-

ing along with me. Please help them to hear You and to understand what You would have them to know and are teaching them.
In Christ Jesus' name I pray,
Amen.

God Is My Provider

> "So Abraham named that place the LORD Provides. Even today people say, 'On the mountain of the LORD it will be provided.'"
> ~Gen. 22:14~

I would like to begin by confessing that for a while I have been trying to decide how I was supposed to start this particular chapter. You see, God really is a good God. But if you have not been walking with Him for very long, it is sometimes hard to realize how good and trustworthy He really is.

Some people find it's so much easier to believe in a God who loves, cares for, and comforts other people. It is easy to believe God to be an all-powerful God in someone else's life, but something totally different when it comes to believing it in our own lives. You see, it can be easy to believe God for others, but it can be so much harder to believe God for ourselves. Sometimes, I guess maybe for fear of being disappointed, we will believe great things from God for other people, but then when it comes time to believe Him for great things in our own lives, we tend to keep God at a distance. And when we believe in a distant God, it's even harder to grasp and believe God will be our provider.

As long as we keep God at a distance, we will continue to rely on ourselves for our provision. From a distant God we can believe for little things. With a distant God we can still believe He exists, and that He has done some mighty things in the past, Jesus is His Son, and that we need to be baptized. With a distant God, that is about it; with everything else, we believe in ourselves. Somewhere we came up with the phrase "God helps those who help themselves," but that is not actually biblical. *Keep in mind that there is also a difference between this and just being lazy. Scripture does warn us about the sin of laziness.*

Part 2: Believing God Is

*<u>JUST FOR CLARITY</u>: We DO have a responsibility to obey God when He gives us directions. **Yes**, there are things only God can do, but when He shows us that we have a certain role that is our part in order to receive His blessings or provisions, then we have a responsibility to respond to His command. For example in Second Kings 4, the widow had to obey and go out and actually get the bottles to fill, BEFORE receiving divine help.*

Going back to what I was talking about at the beginning of this chapter, God doesn't want to be distant to us. He doesn't want to just be "the God in heaven" and us "the people on earth." He doesn't tell us to rely on ourselves and He will see us later. He says over and over again, "I will be your God…depend on me…listen to me…follow me…obey me…." That is not a distant God who expects us to depend on ourselves. He tells us, **"Be still and know that *I am God*"** (Ps. 46:10, emphasis mine).

Before we go to our core verse of Nehemiah 9, I would like to instead turn to Matthew 6:25–26:

> **"So, I tell you, don't worry about the food or drink you need to live, or about the clothes you need for your body. Life is more than food, and the body is more than clothes. Look at the birds in the air. They don't plant or harvest or store food in barns, but your heavenly Father feeds them. And you know that you are worth much more than the birds."**

> God Is My Provider

Then follow on down to verses 32–34: **"The people who don't know God keep trying to get these things. And your Father in heaven knows you need them. Seek first God's kingdom and what God wants. Then all your other needs will be met as well. So don't worry about tomorrow, because tomorrow will have its own worries. Each day has enough trouble of its own."**

If you don't have a close relationship with your almighty God, it will be difficult for you to trust in Him and believe Him to provide for you. I think that is why Jesus says in the verse above, "people who don't know God…" The thing is, though, God wants you to know Him and have a close relationship with Him so you will trust Him, and you will believe Him to provide for you. I also think that is why in the verse above He tells us to "seek first…" because if we are seeking His will for our lives we are focusing on Him and not ourselves. Also, if we are seeking God first, then we are looking to follow His direction and guidance, and we will be doing what it is we were intended to do, in which case, we will be provided for.

In Proverbs 3:5–6 it says, **"Trust the LORD with all your heart, and don't depend on your own understanding. Remember the LORD in all you do, and He will give you success."** In some translations it says, "Lean not on your own understanding…" Psalm 146 talks about God defending widows and orphans. That does support man's theory of "He helps those who help themselves." Sometimes there really is nothing WE can do, but to wait on God for what only HE can do.

When God delivered the Israelites out of Egypt He could have gotten them to the Promised Land in just a matter of days, but they

Part 2: Believing God Is

would have missed out on having to rely on God for their needs and never would have learned this important aspect of God. He does the same for us. Sometimes before giving the blessing He has promised us or the new beginnings He has declared for us, He will take us through seasons where all we can do is rely on Him. But in doing so, we learn so much more about our heavenly Father. Having to depend on Him for our needs teaches us to trust in Him more than ourselves. You can read more about this in Deuteronomy 8:2–5, 15–18.

Core Study Verse: Nehemiah 9:15
"When they were hungry You gave them
bread from heaven. When they were thirsty,
You brought them water from the rock."

My friend, God is not going to take us out of bondage, liberate us from many forms of captivity, and then hang us out to dry. Not if we are following Him, obeying Him, and looking to Him as He has taught us.

Are you familiar with Elijah and his trip to the Kerith Ravine? Read First Kings 17:2–5: **"Then the LORD spoke this word to Elijah: "Leave this place and go east and hide near Kerith Ravine east of the Jordan River. You may drink from the stream, and I have commanded ravens to bring you food there." So Elijah did what the LORD said; he went to Kerith Ravine, east of the Jordan, and lived there. The birds brought Elijah bread and meat every morning and evening, and he drank water from the stream."**

God Is My Provider

The interesting thing about this passage is God said he "commanded." Notice God did not tell Elijah, "Go, and I will command…" or "Go, and this is what I am planning to do…" or even, "Go, and this is what I am thinking of doing…" God said He had *commanded*. That means God had already taken care of this need for food. He had already made provisions. Before Elijah had arrived there, had become hungry and needed the food, God had already supplied. Before the need was ever a "need," God had already taken care of this for Elijah, and all Elijah had to do was trust God would be faithful to His Word and provide what He Himself had promised. Elijah had to take God at His Word and trust that the provisions God had already promised would in fact be there.

This is an awesome reminder that God is all-knowing. He already knew what Elijah would need before he ever got to Kerith Ravine. Before God had even commanded Elijah to "GO," God knew what was already there—the stream—but, He also knew what would be missing—the food—so God provided.

This also teaches us that if God tells us to "GO" we can trust He has already scouted out the area, knows what is there, knows what we will need, and will make provisions for us. The place God is sending us to may be "unknown territory" for us, but God has gone forward, in front of us, to see what is ahead.

But again, as I stated at the beginning of this chapter, if we don't have a close relationship with God, it's hard to trust Him for this. If some stranger told you to go someplace you had never been before and not to worry because he had already provided and it was coming by delivery of some ravens, would you be so willing to go and trust this source? I don't know about you, but I would be hard pressed to do so.

Part 2: Believing God Is

I personally have come to appreciate the Israelites' command to go out and gather each day what they needed when God sent down the manna. The Israelites were told to only take what they needed each day. You see, God wanted them to rely on His certainty each day. It is a lesson for us that hits home in the verse from Matthew 6 we read just a minute ago about not worrying about tomorrow until tomorrow.

A while back I was telling you about my "crossing." What I want to expand on is that I had a very good job. The people were really nice and the hours were flexible, but for reasons I only now understand, I could never "settle in." Let me repeat, it was a good job; it came about when I really needed work. The people there were really good to me and my family. But something inside me sometimes would just ache. I could never quite get comfortable. And I seemed to always be at odds with someone I really liked and appreciated.

The more I tried to get established there, the more it just seemed like "my soul hurt" (is the only way I can describe it). The pay was good; it should have been a place I could have stayed for years! That was my plan and there was no reason not to. I was good at what I did, the management liked my work, and I always received bonuses. So, again, there was no reason from my human perspective to have the constant strife and unsettled feelings I was dealing with.

But as I have already said, now I understand, so let me explain why. God had no designs or desires for me to stay there! God would not allow me to settle in and get comfortable! He had plans for me (and my family) and wanted me to go all the way through my desert and across my Jordan River. I realize now it must have been the same for the Israelites. Could you imagine God's reaction if, after crossing the Red Sea, the Israelites had set up camp with an attitude of, "Okay, thank you very much for setting us free, we'll just set up camp here and settle down. No need to go any further...." I DON'T

> **God Is My Provider**

think God would have calmly agreed. It probably would have been more like, "ARE YOU KIDDING ME? AFTER WHAT I JUST DID? *MOVE!*"

I sometimes have to remind myself there were two bodies of water they had to cross. One coming out of slavery and one going into their Promised Land, and every step of the way in between was a learning experience for them. With each step, they were changing, growing, and learning to walk with God.

That was the same with me. Well, not just me, but my whole family. God had plans for us, a purpose for us, and me getting comfortable in a place—I now realized was just part of my walk—was not what God had in mind. I thought by taking that job I was there to stay. I didn't realize it was just God's way of providing for us until His bigger plan came into play. Hence the reason my spirit just seemed so unsettled. God's Holy Spirit was working in me, and I didn't even know it. But also, when God's timing was coming about for His bigger plan for us, I was having a hard time even thinking about leaving because there was security there. God, however, was not going to mess around. When it came time to move, He really meant MOVE, and He made sure I didn't really have any choice, hence the explosion I talked about earlier. Keep in mind that had I not looked to God's guidance and followed God's prompting where He was trying to lead me, you wouldn't be reading this now.

I can tell you from my own experience, taking a leap of faith and taking God at His Word and trusting Him every day, every step of the way, was really scary at first. I believed in God, but this was going to bring me to a whole new level in my relationship with Him. I can tell you, God has provided. God has taught not just me, but my whole family what it means to really walk with Him and to trust Him. And our reward? Having experiences with God that I will treasure for a lifetime.

Part 2: Believing God Is

I would like to share with you that, a little while back, I was turning into our driveway after picking up our youngest son from school. I was so humbled by a statement he made while I was turning the car off. *"Have you noticed how much better our life is now that we have God? We may not always have a lot of extra stuff, but we seem to always have what we need. I like our life now."* My friend, that came from my ten-year-old son! If a child can learn this amazing lesson from God, then maybe there is hope for each of us! I certainly hope so.

In closing of God Is My Provider,

♥ **PRAYING IN FAITH**

Father God, thank You for this time spent with You. Lord God, thank You for Your provisions and for being our provider. Lord, we praise You because You know all of our needs, even the ones that we don't or can't see. Thank You, that You promise to take care of us and to watch over us, as we look toward You. Lord we praise You for being so patient with us when we are searching for You and trying to understand what steps to take. Thank You that You reach down and hold our hand. Thank You for Your light that You give us to show us the way to go. Lord, we praise You for Your faithfulness in taking care of us. Lord God, I pray also for this reader. I pray that as they grow closer in their walk with You, that they also will be able to witness to others of Your faithfulness in providing for Your children's needs.
In Christ Jesus' name I pray,
Amen.

> "In the beginning You made the earth, and Your hands made the skies. They will be destroyed, but You will remain. They will all wear out like clothes. And, like clothes, You will change them and throw them away. But You never change and Your life will never end."
> ~Ps. 102:25-27~

Section Break II

The incredible thing about God is that there is so much to Him and about Him. If you look at anything in nature—wild birds, for example—there is a very large variety. People are the same way. We can be related to each other and have many similarities yet be so different. But God will be for each of us what we individually need.

You can't put God in a box. If you do, then you downsize Him, and that isn't God. I think that is why I love looking at the sky. It doesn't matter if it is clear, a few clouds, or even overcast; the sky to me is a constant reminder that God is a huge God. I can be looking outside, and it can be crystal clear where I am at, but a family member can call me from where they are in a different town and comment on the rain clouds they see. Different, yet what each place needs. Where we may need sunshine, they may need the rain. So different yet still the same and from the same creator. However, we have to remember to appreciate the beauty of the skies, but

Part 2: Believing God Is

worship God and not things of the sky. (See Deuteronomy 4:19.)

In this next section of our studies in Nehemiah 9, we will look at God as our: *Teacher, Healer, Peace, Wisdom, and Companion.*

We will also look at some characteristics of God, including that He is: *Loyal, Good, Truth, Friend, Stable, and the Living God.*

<u>Core Study Verse: Nehemiah 9:16–21</u>

**"But our ancestors were proud and stubborn
and did not obey Your commands.
They refused to listen; they forgot the miracles You
did for them. So they became stubborn and turned
against You, choosing a leader to take them back to
slavery. But You are a forgiving God. You are kind
and full of mercy. You do not become angry quickly,
and You have great love. So You did not leave
them. Our ancestors even made an idol of
a calf for themselves. They said, 'This is your god,
Israel, who brought you up out of Egypt.'
They spoke against You. You have great mercy,
so You did not leave them in the desert.
The pillar of cloud guided them by day,
and the pillar of fire led them at night,
lighting the way they were to go.
You gave Your good Spirit to teach them.
You gave them manna to eat and water when they
were thirsty. You took care of them for forty years
in the desert; they needed nothing. Their clothes
did not wear out, and their feet did not swell."**

♥ **PRAYING IN FAITH**

Father God, as we continue our study, I praise You for Your greatness. Lord God, Your love for us continues to amaze me. Father God, how I thank You for this time with You. I ask that You will fill us with spiritual wisdom and understanding as this reader and I continue to seek You out. Lord God, I pray that we will come to an even deeper understanding of You and Your will for us and Your call on our lives as we explore Your words together.
Praise You Father God, Holy One of Israel.
In Christ Jesus' name I pray,
Amen

> "I will bring them back, and they will live in Jerusalem. They will be My people, and I will be their good and loyal God."
> ~Zech. 8:8~

God Is Loyal

*T*he first thing I would like to look at in this chapter isn't so much a name but a characteristic of God. You see, I saw something very surprising one afternoon while reading my Bible. Look, if you will, at Numbers 23:20–21: **"He told me to bless them, so I cannot change the blessing. He has found no wrong in the people of Jacob; He saw no fault in Israel."** What had happened in this chapter is an enemy nation tried to hire a prophet to place a curse on the nation of Israel. But when the prophet Balaam came out and looked down over the area where the Israelites were camped, he told the enemy leaders he could only repeat what God's words were concerning the Israelites. The bottom line was this: if God didn't curse the Israelites, then Balaam couldn't either. Hence the verse, "God has found no wrong with the people. "

The first time I read this, I was stunned. In fact, I had to reread Numbers 23 several times as I wanted to make sure I understood it correctly. But, that is what it says. I was a little outraged, on God's behalf. *"He found no wrong?"* I found myself looking at my Bible and asking, "Do you have the right people? You mean the same Israelites who…" I was speechless and didn't know what to think. I mean, just look at the beginning of our core verse of Nehemiah 9:16 for starters.

Part 2: Believing God Is

Core Study Verse: Nehemiah 9:16
"But our ancestors were proud and stubborn and did not obey Your commands. They refused to listen; they forgot the miracles You did for them. So they became stubborn and turned against You, choosing a leader to take them back to slavery."

You mean *THOSE* Israelites? I quickly turned over to Exodus 32, and these are the same Israelites who fashioned a golden calf together and worshiped it, calling it their god when they got worried Moses was up on the mountain with the real GOD getting instructions for them and was taking too long!

In fact, if you flip over to the next chapter, Exodus 33, you will read God told Moses to continue with the travel plans. They were to go where the Lord was leading them. God would still clear a path for them and dispose of the enemy but He Himself would not travel with them. He would send an angel instead because, **"You are a stubborn people, if I were to go with you for even a moment, I would destroy you"** (Exod.33: 5).

I have to tell you this reminds me of my mother. One time when my brothers and I were younger, we made my mother so mad she sent us to our rooms with a loud, "I DON'T CARE IF THE HOUSE IS BURNING DOWN, DON'T COME OUT." Later my brothers just laughed; they knew what she really needed was some time to cool down. However, it bothered me and I must say that it hurt my feelings. So I consoled myself with, "Well, I will never do or say that to my kids."

I shared with you earlier that God has blessed me with boys, three to be exact! So at this point I would really like to be able to say

> God Is
> Loyal

that my kids have not made me eat my words, but that would be lying and I don't want to get struck by lightning while I sit here.

Several years ago, I don't even remember what caused the meltdown, but the boys hit my last nerve. And let me tell you, I sent them packing to their rooms. *No, I didn't say the words*, but I think I had bite marks on my tongue for about a week from my efforts to hold them back. The boys were pretty sure their last meal was coming, and they thought I had sent them to their rooms in punishment. But the truth was I was so upset with them I was afraid I would ultimately say something that would be very hurtful and I didn't want them to perish in my anger. So I mainly sent them to their rooms to get them away from me, to give me space from them, so I could calm down and not do anything or say anything that later I would seriously regret. So I can understand Exodus 33:5.

I went out on the back patio to simmer down. I wasn't about to call my mother and admit my meltdown! However, I called my grandmother. I can remember I sat there on the back step with the phone to my ear and head bent down for several minutes as my grandmother died laughing at my confession. I also had to tell her that I didn't know what made me madder—what the boys had done or the fact they had finally pushed my buttons to the point that "I had become my mother." (Before you start to wonder, YES, I really do love my mom.) I was just furious that my kids had pushed me to my last nerve and all I could think in my mind was, *"Go to your room, and I don't care if..."*

I have to tell you, my thought wasn't so much "DON"T come out." It was more like, *"There is a window so use it if you have to, but stay out of my space..."* I have had to since apologize to my mom for not understanding all those years ago. What I have learned and appreciated even more is the understanding that God was actually protecting His people from His anger. He was mad, YES. But there was still a plan to be carried out, and He needed "time to cool down." (At least that is how I like to phrase it.) So in the same way I sent the boys to their rooms so that I could calm down and not do anything I would regret later, God said the Israelites should continue but He would send an angel to travel with them so that they wouldn't all perish. He was protecting them, even in His in anger, just like a parent.

Now you might be wondering what this has to do with God being loyal. Go back to when I first read the verse in Numbers 23. God might have "found no wrong with them," but I certainly did. I kept wondering how in the world the Bible could say God had found no wrong with these people who over and over again kept turning away from Him? But then God Himself convicted me. In the quietness of my soul, it was like God was saying, *"If I can forgive them and forget, then who are you to try to remind me?"* I was very humbled by this and was very contrite. If God could forgive them and hold to His promise to bless them, then who was I to judge them?

I was reminded that God's thoughts are much higher than ours, and then it was like God was reminding me He had plans not only for an individual, but for a whole nation. The verse in Numbers 23 wasn't talking about the blessing of an individual and that is who God had found no fault with, it was talking about the whole family, the entire nation.

Had there been some "bad apples" among them? Yes, and those individuals were separated and punished. They never made it to the Promised Land, and they never received God's blessings. But the nation did. The "whole" did. God was loyal to His people and faithful to His promise to Abraham. God may have gotten mad and had the whole "go to your room" syndrome, but when "push came to shove" and an enemy tried to say something bad about God's people and

God Is Loyal

curse them, God turned around and said, "Not so fast, those are *My* people."

Again it reminds me of me and my brothers. I am the oldest, and growing up my younger brothers would aggravate me to no end. I would get so mad at them and sometimes would want to "wring their necks." But if someone else were to have said something against them, that was a whole other issue, and one that didn't sit well with me at all. I could get mad at them and sometimes want to "tar and feather" them, but watch me switch gears quickly if someone else came up and wanted to strike out against them. They were "my people," aggravations and all. I loved them and would be loyal to them.

So often God's own people turned against Him, forgot Him, and worshiped false idols. Individuals were punished and disciplined. But as for God's people, as a whole, God was merciful and forgiving to them and remained loyal. Another really nice passage to read about this characteristic of God is Psalm 89; it talks about God's loyalty to David. We won't go there today, but at some point in your quiet time you should read it.

The remaining part of our core verse is
Nehemiah 9:17
"But You are a forgiving God.
You are kind and full of mercy. You do not become angry quickly, and You have great love.
So You did not leave them."

If God can be this forgiving and merciful to the people He loved, even though over and over again they upset Him, shouldn't we learn from His example and do the same? I would like to leave you with one more passage of Scripture to read and consider before we close this chapter. It is from Rom. 9:22–24: **"It is the same way with God. He wanted to show His anger and to let people see His power. But He patiently stayed with those people He was angry with people who were made ready to be destroyed. He waited with patience so that He could make known His rich glory to the people who received His mercy. He has prepared these people to have His glory, and we are those people whom God called."**

In closing of God Is Loyal,

♥ **PRAYING IN FAITH**

Father God, thank You that You are so merciful and loving to us Your children. God, we praise You for Your wonder and patience that You extend to us so often.

Lord God, again thank You for this time spent in Your Word. Lord, I continue to pray for this reader who is reading along and studying with me. Lord God, I pray that You will bless them and be with them. I pray that as they are spending time getting to know You that Your relationship with them is growing.
In Christ Jesus' name I pray,
Amen.

> "I spoke to the prophets and gave them many visions, Through them, I taught My lessons to you."
> ~Hosea 12:10~

God Is My Teacher

I believe there is a reason why the Bible was only written one time and needed to be only so long, with no need to keep adding to it. That is because it doesn't matter what age we live in or what generation we belong to, at some point, we as humans tend to make the same kind of mistakes over and over again. So the same principle lessons that were taught to the people of the Bible so long ago are the same principle lessons we still need to learn today. A good verse for you to look up and read that goes along with this thought, is Ecclesiastes 3:15, **"What happens now has happened in the past, and what will happen in the future has happened before."**

Thankfully we in the new covenant of Christ don't have to make the same blood offerings that the generations in Moses' time had to. But the same key lessons God wanted His people to learn about Him are still the same. Also, if you will pray for an open mind and a learning heart before reading your Bible you will see the Holy Spirit showing you similarities in your situation and the circumstances in your life to that of the people in biblical times. The same lessons that God sought to teach His people then are what He wants to teach you and me now.

Jesus told His followers in Matthew 24:35, **"Earth and sky will be destroyed, but the words I have said will never be destroyed."** Just as God Himself will not change, neither does His Word. If God will go to great lengths to teach His people back then, we have to know that He will do that for us now. He is going to have to, otherwise how will we be able to grow and walk with Him? In the same way that we cannot expect our children to go outside and work on something if we haven't taught them how, God teaches us how to follow Him.

The other evening one of the tenants who is leasing an office suite in our building called because his air conditioner wasn't working. Instead of calling the service technicians out, our oldest son said he would go up and look at it. An hour and a half later, he had it working just fine and our tenant was very happy and kept commending our son on a job well done. Now, our son could never have done that if he hadn't been taught how.

Throughout this study I keep stressing my desire for you to look up the Scriptures for yourselves and take time to read them. It's not because I don't have confidence in what I am sharing with you, but because I want you to enjoy a rich, full relationship of your own with God and not a secondhand relationship through me or my experiences.

Imagine if someone came up to you saying, "Hey, God has granted me one request and I have asked for Peter to come down and teach you personally." Now, that would be wonderful. Just think of learning under someone like Peter who actually walked and talked with Jesus! But what if I came to you and said, "Well, Jesus decided that wasn't quite good enough, so He has decided to come down and teach you personally." Who would you rather learn firsthand from -- Peter or Jesus?

Keep in mind I am in NO WAY comparing myself to Peter; I am just using that as an analogy. What I am ultimately trying to say is: use what I am sharing with you as a tool and a stepping stone, then dig deeper into God's Word and experience how God will bring His words to life in your heart and in your circumstances. Then later as

God Is My Teacher

you come alongside someone, you will be able to say, "This is what God has taught me."

Core Study Verse: Nehemiah 9:19-20

"You have great mercy, so You did not leave them in the desert. The pillar of cloud guided them by day, and the pillar of fire led them at night, lighting the way they were to go. You gave Your good Spirit to teach them. You gave them manna to eat and water when they were thirsty."

Why did God do these things? (1) To provide for them, and (2) To teach them. By doing these things He taught them about Himself. He showed them that He was faithful, that He cared for them, that He was strong enough to protect them…all the things we have been reading and talking about already in this book and still everything else to come. God taught them who He was, which is what this whole study book is about.

In the Old Testament, God taught His people through priests and leaders He chose who had an open mind and heart in which to hear God's words. Listen to what Moses told the people in Deuteronomy 30:11–14: **"This command I give you today is not too hard for you; it is not beyond what you can do. It is not up in heaven. You do not have to ask, 'Who will go up to heaven and get it for us so we can obey it and keep it?' It is not on the other side of the sea. You do not have to ask, 'Who will go across the sea and get it? Who will tell it to us so we can keep it?' No, the word is very near you. It is in your mouth and in your heart so you may obey it."**

What the Israelites didn't know was Moses was referring to God's Holy Spirit who would be sent to live inside of future generations. However, because Christ hadn't come yet and died, God's Holy Spirit hadn't been released. Moses was trying to teach the people that God's Word and God Himself were not far away and He would be released inside of people to come. My Friend, that is us!

When we accept Christ, God's Holy Spirit comes to live inside of us so the spirit in us can commune with God. It is through the Spirit of God that we are able to learn, heed His voice, and follow Him.

Jesus explained to His followers that although He was at the moment speaking to them, later there would be another sent to them. The Holy Spirit was to help them remember what Jesus had taught them previously and also to continue teaching them of things to come. My friend, the same Spirit lives in us! That same Spirit that Jesus spoke of helps us to learn and recall what God has said to us. John 14:25–26 says, **"I have told you all these things while I am with you. But the Helper will teach you everything and will cause you to remember all that I told you. This Helper is the Holy Spirit whom the Father will send in My name."**

So in saying all of that, I encourage you to open your heart to God's Holy Spirit. Let Him come in and take up residence inside of you. Invite the Holy Spirit to renew your mind and thinking, to clean out old or wrong understanding and give you new perspective and knowledge of God Himself. In doing so, it is truly eye-opening, and I don't just mean your human eyes, but your spiritual eyes as well. Ask God; invite Him to give you a desire to learn. Ask God to teach you how. I have never known or heard of God turning an invitation like that down.

Another lesson on God being our teacher involves God taking someone aside to help them. The first verse I ask you to turn to is

The Very Heart of Worship

God Is My Teacher

Mark 7:33, **"Jesus led the man away from the crowd, by himself. He put His fingers in the man's ears and then spit and touched the man's tongue."**

Now, why the need to take the man away from the crowd? I think it was to take the man away from all those who would distract him into unbelief. By taking the man away, all he could do was focus on Jesus. The Lord now would have his undivided attention. Remember, it is our belief that God can and will help us that brings divine action.

This is the same concept as with the man and his little girl in Mark 5:35–36: **"While Jesus was still speaking, some people came from the house of the synagogue leader. They said, 'Your daughter is dead. There is no need to bother the teacher anymore.' But Jesus paid no attention to what they said. He told the synagogue leader, 'Don't be afraid; just believe.'"**

Put yourself in this man's shoes. Someone just tells you your daughter is dead, but here is a flicker of hope from someone else saying, "No, she's not." Think of the turmoil he must have felt, torn between human feelings of wanting to crumble at what the physical circumstances looked like and a heart-wrenching hope that maybe it's not what it appears to be. When everyone came up to this man saying, "Your daughter is dead," for the briefest of moments his face turns to look at them. Jesus looks him straight in the eye and says, "NO! Don't look at them, Look at me. Don't listen to them, listen to me. Don't believe them, BELIEVE ME."

Think of the courage it must have taken for this man to turn his back on everything human logic would say is true so he could dare to believe what Jesus was saying instead. I wonder if it took a second, if there was the slightest pause while this man stood, among his family and friends who were crying and mourning, and stared into Jesus' face. Imagine, two pair of eyes searching each other's, one pair of eyes pleading, "Trust me, believe me," and the other pair of eyes in tears searching for the hope of possibilities. I wonder how long they stood there. I wonder how long it took for this man to make his decision. Was it in the space of a heartbeat, maybe? Or, was it just long enough for him to take a deep breath and work up the courage to take a step forward?

However long, I guess it doesn't matter because Scripture shows his faith was enough. The next verses show that somewhere inside this man, he believed. Jesus left with this man, Peter, James, and John, and when they arrived at this man's house only to be met with ridicule and laughter, Jesus threw everyone out. And again, "He took aside in private" only those with faith to believe. And this little girl and her parents received God's gift of resurrection.

These aren't the only times that Jesus took people aside. Another viewpoint of this is that Jesus often took His disciples aside to teach them and to share with them things to come and to explain in private the lessons He had taught openly among many others. Matthew 20:17, Mark 10:32 and Luke 9:10 are some examples of this.

If you put this into the perspective of our core study verse from Nehemiah 9, we see the same thing during Moses' time. Turn to Exodus 24:12–18. God called Moses up on the mountain to spend time with Him so He could teach Moses and give him instructions to take back to the whole group. You see, God needed time alone with Moses so that Moses could focus on God's voice and obtain God's Word without the distractions of leadership responsibilities and the clamoring of all the people.

> **God Is My Teacher**

When God calls you aside to spend time with Him, don't struggle against Him. Know that at some point He is going to send you back down to the people. But for a season, enjoy the time with God and the incredible knowledge that God, the awesome wonder of the universe, wants you to Himself.

Remember though, God never blesses us or gives us something for greed's sake. He expects us to share. He blesses one so others may receive as well. It could be financial blessings, material blessings, or even the Word of God. I like Matt. 10:27, **"I tell you these things in the dark, but I want you to tell them in the light. What you hear whispered in your ear you should shout from the housetops."** He teaches us so that in return we can share it and teach someone else for Him.

In closing of God is My Teacher,

♥ PRAYING IN FAITH

Father God, thank You. We praise You for Your willingness to teach us. Thank You for Your lessons and for Your Holy Spirit who helps us to learn. Lord, as much as You are willing, we ask You to pour out spiritual wisdom and knowledge into each of us. Lord, show us and share with us Your truths. Teach us to walk in Your way. Teach us to live according to Your plans that You have for each of us.

Lord God, thank You for this time spent in Your Word. Lord, I pray that Your words are being planted and growing in this reader's life as well.
In Christ Jesus' name I pray,
Amen.

> "Give thanks to the LORD because He is good. His love continues forever."
> ~Ps. 136:1~

God Is Good

Another characteristic of God I would like to look at is that God is good. Even when we are in the midst of chaos, if we will just take the time to refocus, we will see God is just waiting to give us something good to look at. I have found that if I will take the time to look at the glory of God, then my struggle or situation suddenly doesn't seem nearly as big. It becomes downsized and isn't the giant I once thought it was. I have found that in the midst of "Oh, God please..." I find something to be thankful for. I may make requests of my God in the morning, but in the evening, as I look back at the day from God's perspective and see the traces of His hand, then I always have something to be thankful for.

A long time ago, our family started what we call our "good, bad, and funny." Usually it's dinner time when we do this. One of us will start by asking someone else, "What is the worst thing that happened to you today?" We always start with the bad thing first, so that way whatever difficulty we went through is acknowledged and discussed but we don't dwell upon it. Then the next thing asked is, "Okay, what was the best thing that happened to you today?" And then we discuss it. After which, whoever started us off for the evening will ask the same person, "What was your funny thing today, what made you laugh?" Then whoever just finished telling us about their day will pick someone else. And this will continue until all of us have had a turn.

It is amazing how I can pick up one of my sons from school and as they get into the car, I can ask them how their day was and hear, "It was okay." But then that night the same day that was only "okay" comes to life and I find out all kinds of things. Even from our teenager! What is also nice is it produces conversation and interaction between the boys that a moment earlier wasn't there. Sometimes it is as simple as one of us saying we didn't have anything bad happen and that in turn becomes the good thing! It was really nice when, a while back, our oldest son had a really rotten day, so we discussed it (yes, we do put time limits on this) and then our youngest son asked, "Well, what was your good thing?" Our oldest one replied, "Being here as a family having dinner and doing our 'good, bad, and funny.'" And sometimes one of us won't have a funny thing to share until we've heard someone else's.

What is so awesome is as we can say our goodnight prayers; often I will listen to my youngest son pray in such childlike fashion and faith thanking God for something his brother shared with us at dinner time. Or sometimes we will sit and listen as he discusses with God an issue one of his brothers is going through that was revealed at dinner.

During a really turbulent time a while back I bought a nice notebook with a special pen and I only write prayers of thanksgiving in it. I may journal all my other woes and "this and that" along with my thank yous in a daily journal, but in this notebook—though I may not write in it every day—I only write positive, thankful praises to God in it. I have found it helps to put the focus on God instead of myself.

I have come to appreciate the prayer in Habakkuk 3:17–18: **"Fig trees may not grow figs, and there may be no grapes on the vines. There may be no olives growing and no food growing in the fields. There may be no sheep in the pens and no cattle in the barns. But I will still be glad in the LORD; I will rejoice in the God my Savior."**

> **God Is Good**

An example of God's goodness I would like to share is an answered prayer for our middle son. I have already written about it in complete detail in another book, so I won't repeat it here but I will summarize it for you. About two years ago my son was able to see something I couldn't. He had texted me to hurry and go outside and look up at the sky. So I dropped what I was doing and went to look, but all I saw were the remaining rain clouds from the spring shower we just had.

In our texted conversation back and forth, he told me he could see a double rainbow, almost from end to end. I replied that from where I was at I wasn't able to see it. A minute or two later, he texted asking me to please stop whatever I was doing, just close my eyes and be still. So I did, and then he texted me asking if I had "seen it." I found out he had been staring intently at this beautiful scene and was praying somehow God would give me the vision he could see but that I was missing.

Three days later, I'd left work but had to go back and pick up something I had forgotten and some of the men were there. In the course of a conversation with one of my bosses, it came up that one of our truck drivers had been on the other side of town and took a picture of the double rainbow my son had seen. After going out to the bay and visiting with this truck driver he showed me the picture he had taken, and I want to tell you that the date and time that were on the picture were the exact time my son was asking me to close my eyes and be still!

Fortunately, I hadn't deleted the text messages yet, so I was able to go back and look at the message from my son telling me to please stop what I was doing and close my eyes. The time on my phone matched the time printed on the picture this man had taken. I was able to show it to him just to prove it. He then sent me a copy of the photo and when I was able to pick up my son later, I had a surprise for him! The look on his face and his expression of "God really did answer my prayer!" was more priceless to me than the photo of the rainbows.

To me the incredible and awesome extent which God worked in order to fulfill my son's prayer and enable me to have "the vision" he could see and I was missing is something that could only come from a loving and GOOD God. It was also a nice lesson for both of us, that at the same time my son was praying, God had indeed answered him, but it took a few days to reach me. Read Daniel 10:12–13:

> **"Then the man said to me, 'Daniel, do not be afraid. Some time ago you decided to get understanding and to humble yourself before your God. Since that time God has listened to you, and I have come because of your prayers. But the prince of Persia has been fighting against me for twenty-one days. Then Michael, one of the most important angels, came to help me. I had been left there with the king of Persia.'"**

At the time Daniel started praying, God answered, but it took three weeks before Daniel received his answer. Sometimes the very thing we are praying for, God has already given us. We just have to know that sometimes the enemy will fight tooth and nail to keep it from us. But if it is what God would have for us, then God will overcome. Our job is to keep praying and believing that God is good and He will ultimately come through for us, though it may be in a completely unexpected way.

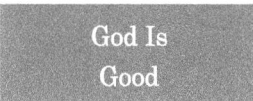

This reminder brings us back to our core study verse:

Core Study Verse: Nehemiah 9:21
"You took care of them for forty years in the desert; they needed nothing. Their clothes did not wear out, and their feet did not swell."

God took care of His people. He didn't leave them. He didn't forget about them, and He didn't ignore their needs while they were traveling. At times were they disciplined and punished? Yes, but He still provided and watched over them. Really it is no different for us as parents. Even though our children get into trouble, we aren't going to stop fulfilling our parental duties.

From the very beginning God has done this for mankind. He was the one to shed blood on our behalf. Even after Adam and Eve ignored Him and disregarded His commands, when it came time to send them out of the Garden, God took one look at what they were wearing and said it would never do. So he clothed them. (See Genesis 3:21.) Just as God is the beginning and the end of all things, He was here also. He began by shedding blood from an animal to clothe us naturally and then shed blood from His Son to clothe us spiritually. I believe that from the very beginning even until now, God has been, is, and forever will be, good to us. Even when we do not always deserve it, I believe we can trust God will be good to us.

In closing of God is Good,

♥ **PRAYING IN FAITH**

Father God, thank You. Lord, we praise You for being such a good and loving God. Thank You, too, for Your patience with us even when we are so undeserving. Lord, thank You for what Your Word teaches us about You. We praise You, Lord, for Your love that is everlasting.

Father, I pray that over the course of this study, this reader will come to see Your good and powerful handprints on their lives as they come to know You deeper still.
In Christ Jesus' name I pray,
Amen.

> "God's word is true and everything He does is right. He loves what is right and fair; the LORD'S love fills the earth."
> ~Ps. 33:4–5~

God Is Truth

When looking at the time our core chapter of Nehemiah 9 relates to, we find it is the journey of the Israelites from the time they left Egypt until they arrived in the Promised Land. However, I would like to point out that before this journey ever started, God told Moses specific details that would prove to be true.

Turn to Exodus 3:18–22. While Moses' head was still reeling from the bombshell God had just announced to him, God was giving Moses a preview of things to come. *"The elders will listen to you...But I know that the king of Egypt will not let you go...In this way you will take with you the riches of the Egyptians."* And then, of course we know that every bit of this happened.

Throughout the Israelites' travels, God continually forewarned them. God even told Moses about the Israelites losing heart. Read Deuteronomy 5:28–29. Here again, we know that what God foretold indeed came to pass.

I would like to take you on a quick detour to something that hit me profoundly from Scripture in Jeremiah 1:19: **"They will fight against you, but they will not defeat you, because I am with you to protect you!' says the LORD."** What I would like to quickly point out to you is that God told Jeremiah from the very beginning that people would fight against him. God was letting Jeremiah know beforehand that life was going to be rough for him. However, God promised to be with him and protect him, and He did. For example, when Jeremiah was thrown down a well and left for dead, God sent someone to save him. God did not leave him there. You might want to argue both sides of the coin that Jeremiah died a very sad death. Yes, he did, but only after his work was done. God kept him and watched over Jeremiah until his mission was completed and only then did he go home to be with God.

You also have to remember that Jeremiah's purpose and message from God wasn't just for the people of his day, it was for us as well. Many of the prophets, Ezekiel, for example, were not welcomed, treated well, or believed by the people of their day. But it wasn't just for them. What these men were preaching might have fallen on deaf ears around them, but God had a greater plan. God knew the message these men spoke back then would stand the test of time and be given to us as well. Whenever God is working through us, it is never for us alone. God intends for His work, and His Word, in us to spread way beyond our common ground.

Go back, if you will, to Numbers 23:19: **"God is not a human being, and He will not lie. He is not a human, and He does not change His mind. What He says He will do, He does. What He promises, He makes come true."** This is such a strong verse to hold onto when you are going through difficult times and it seems as if you are never going to make it to your destination. I encourage you to write this verse down, begin your prayers with it, and meditate on it. Dear friend, the sheer fact that Jesus was born and then died on the cross shows us that when God has said something, even if it takes years to come to pass, we can bank on it.

Whenever God speaks to your heart—if you have truly had a word or message from God about your circumstances—then know that when the LORD has spoken no one can take those words away from you. They will be done.

The Very Heart of Worship

God Is Truth

The problem we (as humans) tend to have is that a majority of the time, our timetable is not God's. So often, if what we believe God has shared with us doesn't happen instantly, we start to drift off and fall into unbelief. In the same way paper can become yellow with age, our mental grasp of God's Word can yellow and age as time passes if we allow it.

My friend, pray and claim God's promise: "Call to me and I will answer you and show you things to come..." Acknowledge the lifeline of hope God gives you, pray over the answer you believe you have received, and if need be, ask for and then watch for confirmation. Afterward, I strongly suggest you journal God's answer and His confirmation, especially if they come to you in different ways. Remember, God does communicate with us, but it can be in a variety of ways. So again, journal it, write it down, and go out in the yard to find a "memory stone" so that if your promise does indeed take time to cultivate and bear fruit, then you have a firm substance to hold onto and stand on. Don't let the enemy, in any form, take God's Word from you; stand firm on what God tells you. God cannot and does not lie.

Know that when God promises blessing, then in due time blessings come. However, in the same manner, when God determines punishment and discipline, He delivers! He is not like a parent that says, "Now son, if you do that one more time..." and then fails to keep His Word. What God says, God does. God is not a "maybe" kind of God. He doesn't tell us He will think about it or "Well, maybe, I might...." When God says yes, He means yes. But when our all-powerful God says no, then He means no. A good verse to look up and mark in our Bibles is Second Corinthians 1:17–22. When Paul's plans changed he was worried that people might think his word wasn't reliable. He hadn't made plans and then on a whim decided, "Oh well, I will just do something else instead." Paul goes on to say that you can believe God and that God is not a double-minded God.

When reading in the Gospels, we frequently see Jesus quoting Scripture (see Matthew 4). Even in His dying moments He relied on Scripture. I stated a moment ago that His birth and death proves Scripture to be true. But Jesus went even further and proved it by bringing to pass many things that were written about Him hundreds of years earlier! Jesus went above and beyond anything imaginable just to show us that we could count on and believe the Word of God. I personally think one of the most compelling Scriptures about Jesus in the Old Testament is Isaiah 53:7–8. Whenever I read it, I am so touched that such an incredible portrait of Jesus was given to people long before He was born. I appreciate the way it describes Him and the death He would face for us because it really happened. What the prophets heard God tell them to write down for everyone to read and see amazes me and captures my heart.

And like Father, like Son. Jesus did what God did. So often Jesus made it a point to tell His followers exactly what was going to happen. A prime example is Jesus telling Peter that even though Peter was professing a stand in faith, it wouldn't stand the test of time. And again, just like with His Father, time proved Jesus' words to be true.

Turn to Luke 2. The shepherds were told about the birth of Jesus. I love verse 15:

> **"Let's go to Bethlehem.**
> **Let's see this thing that has happened which**
> **the Lord has told us about."**

The Very Heart of Worship

God Is Truth

So off they went. Now look at verse 20: **"The shepherds went back to their sheep, praising God and thanking Him for everything they had seen and heard. It had been just as the angel had told them."**

Dear friend, any time God's Word comes to pass for you to see it, any time God does something (even minor) so that you will know it was Him, PLEASE remember to take the time to turn and acknowledge it and thank Him. Please don't ever take even the smallest gesture from our Father God for granted. We need to respect Him for several reasons: (1) The fact that the Sovereign Lord of the universe parted heaven to announce His presence is an incredible and awesome thing not to be taken lightly. (2) The more we take notice and recognize God's handprint, the more our eyes will be opened for us to see. The more we see, then the more we will believe, and the more we believe, then the more we will see. (3) The more we acknowledge, the more we can witness, and the more our spiritual relationship with God grows. (4) The more our relationship with Him grows, the more glory we give to God and the more we can help others to know about Him. It always comes full circle.

Another wonderful Scripture to mark and hold onto as you walk with God is Hebrews 6:13–20. To summarize it for you, when we as humans make a promise, many times we will swear it by something as if this gives it more substance and credibility. But God wanted to prove His promise was true so He took an oath on His own name so we would know that God's purposes never change and that He cannot (and will not) lie. We can be sure of two things: (1) when God makes a promise, it will come to pass, and (2) when God makes an oath, it also will come to pass.

Again, though, keep in mind that God's timing is not always our timing and it can take a while for us to see evidence of what God has said. Turn to First Samuel 15. After disobeying God and then trying to pin his disobedience on everyone else, Samuel told Saul, "You don't realize it, but today you just lost your kingdom."

> **"Samuel said to him, 'The LORD has torn the kingdom of Israel from you today and has given it to one of your neighbors who is better than you. The LORD is the Eternal One of Israel. He does not lie or change His mind. He is not a human being, so He does not change His mind'"** (First Sam. 15:28–29).

For all appearances' sake, Saul might have continued to wear a crown on his head, but it was all cosmetic. God immediately sent Samuel to anoint David, God's spirit left Saul, and David went into training. It took quite a few years to see the external evidence of God's Word, but what God said that day was in fact true. In the same way, when we plant a garden we start with seeds. To an outsider passing by it may still look like barren land, but to us, who planted it, we can already see vegetation because we know it's there. We planted the seeds and now all we need to do is water, cultivate them, wait for them, and watch them grow. And for the outsider who has been driving by? Eventually that person will see what we have known all along was there.

Here is one last thought I would like to share with you before closing this chapter. Turn to John 14:15–31 where Jesus told His followers that the Holy Spirit would later be sent to them to help them to remember and understand what they had been taught. Specifically, please look at verse 29:

> **"I have told you this now, before it happens, so that when it happens you will believe."**

The Very Heart of Worship

God Is Truth

I want to share with you that I believe this. I truly believe when you are walking every day in a personal relationship with God, that many times His Holy Spirit will foretell you things so you will be prepared, so that inside, your spirit will know what is coming and will be prepared. I have to tell you that many times I will be reading my Bible and, for whatever reason, a specific passage of Scripture will just leap off the page for me and it's all I can read or even think about.

Then sure enough, over a short period of time, I will see it repeated often in the daily devotionals I read. I have learned when this happens to take the time to really read it over and over so I can absorb it. And every time, something will come up either directly in my circumstances or those of someone I am close to and care about, and what I have learned in the repeated lesson is perfect. I already know which way to go, or the decision to make, or the exact word to share.

One time it wasn't just with Scripture. I was at work and I was filing some papers and ever so briefly, I imagined myself sitting with someone else showing them how to file these things and explaining to them what the files were for and how the payees were sorted. The thought I had was a flashing one and I didn't think anything else about it. But two weeks later, it happened! I was no longer the employee as decisions had been made, and I moved on. But, I was called back and asked to train someone who would be replacing me. Since there were no hard feelings, and I already knew God had been involved in the move, I agreed.

But sitting there that afternoon two weeks later, I was showing someone the files. I was sitting in the exact spot with the same drawer opened showing the filing system to the other person, and all of a sudden I had a wonderful remembrance! Exactly what I had briefly pictured two weeks earlier was coming into play and it gave me such a peaceful feeling. It was as if God was reminding me that He had already shown me this and He had already known this would happen. If I had any lingering doubts or questions, they were laid to rest as God showed me that not only was He aware of this, it was of Him.

In closing of God is Truth,

♥ **PRAYING IN FAITH**

Father God, how wonderful You are. Thank You so much for Your words that You give us. Thank You for teaching us and sharing Your words with us. Thank You that we can stand by them and hold firm to them. Thank You, God, for Your Holy Spirit, who helps us to learn, who helps us to remember what You have told and taught us. We praise You, Lord, for the peace, comfort, and strength that Your truth give us.

Lord, I pray for this reader. Father God, I pray that as they continue with this study, that Your words and Your truths will be planted and rooted deeply into them.
In Christ Jesus' name I pray,
Amen.

> "I no longer call you servants; because a servant does not know what his master is doing. But I call you friends, because I have made known to you everything I heard from Father."
> ~John 15:15~

God Is My Friend

The name I would like to look at now isn't necessarily out of a specific verse from our core chapter of Nehemiah 9, but more of a summary of something deeper I would like to think about with you. When reading through our core study verses something that does stand out is the repeated rebelliousness of the Israelites—the constant griping only shortly after seeing God do something. But, what isn't really highlighted is something about Moses I would like to address: the fact that so often he went to bat for them! Many times Moses put himself between them and God.

So many times he interceded for them and they were unaware of it. Or when they did know, they just didn't seem to understand how much he did for them, so they didn't really appreciate it. Not only did Moses pray on their behalf, but he was willing to lay down his life for them—to trade his life for theirs. When it came to the point where God was willing to destroy them and start over, Moses pleaded in prayer for them, admitting they where a sinful people but reminding God that they were still His people and that he would give his life for theirs. (See Exodus 32:25–35.)

Have you ever been there? Can you relate? Have you ever gone to bat for someone and they had no clue because to them everything worked out fine. But what they didn't know was your role behind the scene. John 15:13 says, **"The greatest love a person can show**

is to die for his friends." And ultimately that is what Jesus did for us.

Sometimes God asks if we care enough to do the same. What He wants to know is, are we willing to lay our lives down for another? Do we love others the way the Bible teaches us to? Can we, or more importantly, do we, show that kind of friendship to others? Our "laying down our life" may not necessarily mean literally dying for others; it can mean interceding for them in prayer. Spending time, not just a minute or two, but caring enough to get alone with God for a significant period of time to pray and intercede on their behalf. This is called heartfelt praying, when you are willing to approach the throne of grace and plead on their behalf.

Or maybe it involves giving up something we wanted for ourselves in order to see someone else blessed. I once read about a man who took someone else's job cut when the company they worked for was going through layoffs. (Talk about friendship and putting someone else first!) The bottom line is, any time we are willing to give up or do something in true heartfelt sacrifice for someone else, we have "laid down for them," we have put someone else's needs above our own. That is what Moses did and this is the example that Christ Himself has given us to follow.

One biblical story often taught is when Moses hit the rock instead of speaking to it as God had commanded and it cost him his trip into the Promised Land. Did he disobey God? Yes! Is there a lesson to be learned in that? YES! But, when Moses died, God Himself buried Moses, and would let no other have a part in it. That is pretty awesome and says a lot right there. Moses might not have made it into the Promised Land, but he went straight to Paradise, so I don't feel overly sorry for him in "not making it."

God Is My Friend

However, this is not one of the lessons I want to talk about. Instead, turn to Numbers 20. The people were once again complaining and griping at Moses and Aaron that there was no water. Once before they had no water and God provided, so why wouldn't God do it again? I'm sorry, but if I had just witnessed even some of the things God had already done on this trip, I think I would be a little careful about how I spoke to God's chosen leader! God told Moses to speak to the rock and there would be water. But after losing his temper Moses hit the rock instead. God told him that, because of this, he lost the right to lead the people into the Promised Land.

Notice anything significant after this and in the following chapters of Numbers or even Deuteronomy? Moses didn't quit! He didn't throw his hands up in the air and do what I know so many other people would do. He didn't throw his staff down and say, "That's it, I have had enough, and you people are on your own." I mean, think about it. He just lost his entrance into the Promised Land. God had just told him he wouldn't be the one to lead them there. But Moses kept with the assignment God gave him. He kept on, and with good leadership. He held to what God wanted him to do all the way until the end. He continued to lead them as best he could and after God told him he was about to die, he still interceded for them one more time.

> **"Moses said to the LORD, 'The LORD is the God of the spirits of all people. May He choose a leader for these people, who will go in and out before them. He must lead them out like sheep and bring them in; the LORD's people must not be like sheep without a shepherd"** (Num. 27:15–17).

Now, I know that so far this has appeared to be about Moses, and our study is supposed to be about God who is our Friend. But, really it is about the friendship between Moses and God. In Exodus 33:11 it says, **"The LORD spoke to Moses face to face as a man speaks with his friend."** Then afterward, Moses had the gumption to ask God to "show me your glory" and God did! Several times we read that Moses was very open about his thoughts and feelings with God. If Moses was upset about something, he told God. But, Moses also dropped to the ground instantly to worship this same God over and over again.

And as I stated earlier, when Moses died it was God, and God alone, who buried him. There is something so intimate and personal in that. Sometimes I think about it and try to imagine how beautiful that moment must have been. Up on the mountaintop overlooking so much, it makes me wonder, was there a breeze? If I had been there would I have heard birds in the trees or maybe just the wind whispering? Did God have the angels sing? When Moses died, it was God's hand that covered him.

God wants to have the same kind of friendship with us. How can I say that? Because of what Jesus did for Paul. Acts 23:11 says, **"The next night the LORD came and stood by Paul. He said, 'Be brave! You have told people in Jerusalem about Me. You must do the same in Rome.'"** Take note, when Paul had to stand and face opposition, God did not expect him to do it alone; the LORD stood by him. Then in Second Timothy 4:14–17 we read, **"The first time I defended myself, no one helped me; everyone left me. May they be forgiven. But the LORD stayed with me and gave me strength so I could fully tell the Good News to all those who are not Jews."**

The Lord's Spirit is with us. Just as He was with Paul, He will be with us. Friend, even when we are in complete despair and don't know what or how we should pray, God's Spirit will intercede for us. Scripture says:

The Very Heart of Worship

God Is My Friend

"Also, the Spirit helps us with our weakness. We do not know how to pray as we should. But the Spirit Himself speaks to God for us, even begs God for us with deep feelings that words cannot explain. God can see what is in people's hearts. And He knows what is in the mind of the Spirit, because the Spirit speaks to God for His people in the way God wants" (Rom. 8:26–27).

Several months ago, my grandmother (on my mother's side) suddenly took a turn for the worse and was dying. When my grandfather called my mother, they didn't even think my mother would make it there in time. Now, you have to know that I come from a pretty good-sized family. My mother has three children, and we all have children, plus I have a step-sister with a baby. My mother has a sister with three children and they have started families, so when we all get together there are quite a few people. But it was my grandmother, out of everyone, I was the closest to.

And when I got the call, I sobbed. She had originally been taken to the hospital a few days earlier for what they thought was pneumonia. However, she wasn't responding to the medicine and by the time my mother got there and was able to call me, it was really bad and there was no hope. My mom said there was nothing they could do, that it wasn't pneumonia, and her cancer had come back this time with a vengeance and was present in the fluid in her lungs, so I sobbed again. But this time, it was with racking sobs. We are talking crying that came from far down in me. For me, it was almost like Mary and Martha sending someone to Jesus saying, "Come quick, the one you love is sick" (see John 11).

You see, my grandmother hadn't been to church in years. I know that at one time she believed there was a God, but that was about it.

151

And what was upsetting me was no one was there, that I knew of, who would go and just pray with her about her salvation.

My grandmother had beaten breast cancer *twice* before and had been cancer free for quite a while. But what the doctors found this time was that fluids throughout her body, and her lungs, were filled with it. In fact, her body was pretty much drowning itself, which made for a very painful and scary death for her and a painful experience for my mother and grandfather watching it. Not to mention that my grandmother was *suffering horribly*. My mother called me on Sunday night to tell me this. And all day Monday I sobbed uncontrollably.

But the amazing thing was that even though I was sobbing on the outside, inside of me I could hear praying. It had to be God's Holy Spirit praying what I couldn't, because I was sobbing for several reasons. For one, there was no way I could get down there to see her before she died, and for another, I was losing someone extremely close to me and she wasn't at peace, but suffering. But most importantly to me was the need to pray with her. I just needed, and wanted so much, to be able to pray with her before she died. So my deepest sobs were that someone would pray with her, and just lead her back to God if she hadn't already reconfirmed her relationship with Him.

The next day, a Tuesday, I called the hospital hoping to be able to talk to my mother (I felt horrible that I couldn't be there for my mom either), and instead I got to talk to my *grandmother*! She was sitting up in bed eating and visiting with everyone in the room! By Wednesday afternoon, the fluids in her lungs were all dried up. Now what I was told was that it must have been due to the morphine they were giving her. It had been decided that since there was NOTHING they could do for her and because she was suffering so much and

God Is My Friend

struggling against "drowning," that they would just give her morphine and try to make her comfortable.

Now, I am no doctor, but I have been in the hospital before and have had to take morphine: "glowing" (which is how I was told my grandmother looked on that Wednesday) and sitting up eating, visiting, and even talking on the phone, is not how I was!

The rest of that week went by, and into the following week the doctors said that at this rate, she could live for possibly another three to six months before the cancer would take her whole body. My mother would text me each day during that week and a half on how well my grandmother was doing. In fact, she tried to send me a picture of my grandmother, but my grandmother put her hand up and said, "Oh no, I don't have on any makeup." So how's THAT for doing pretty well?

However, on Friday of that week, for whatever reason, I started sobbing again. We are talking about "down on the floor, and couldn't get up," kind of sobbing. But inside, again I could hear praying. By 8:30 that night I had to go to bed because my head hurt so incredibly bad. But at 10:30 I woke up. I sat up and was completely wide awake. Two hours later my mother called me to say that the hospital had called them and said my grandmother had died. She would have died about the time I woke up.

I asked my mom what had happened. She said she wasn't really sure, that earlier in the evening she and my grandfather had gone up and had dinner with grandmother. My granddad kissed her goodnight, and a nurse came in to take her vitals and they were fine. It was while the nurse had turned around to get something off the cart that she died. And no, it had not been a heart attack. Her heart had just, literally stopped in a beat. It was very peaceful, and in the middle of a conversation, as the nurse was talking to her and turned around to get something. When she turned back around my grandmother hadn't answered her and at first the nurse thought she had fallen asleep.

Two days later, I was praying and asking God if my grandmother had made it to Him. I was consoling myself with the fact I had no idea how God would ever answer me on that one, and left it as an unanswered prayer. A little while later I was on the phone with my cousin and, in a passing comment from her, I found out that on Friday afternoon, while my mother and grandfather had been out, a pastor from someone's church had come up to visit one of their members, and saw my grandmother in the room by herself, so he went in and sat down to visit and pray with her. From what I was told, he was in there for quite some time. It was shortly after he had left that my grandfather and mother had came back to have dinner with her.

I quickly realized God had a way to answer me after all. He answered that prayer, and the other one as well, as she did not die *until* someone had prayed with her. She didn't die the next day or two after the pastor's visit. She died *that same evening* after someone had prayed with her. I am thoroughly convinced that on Monday when the fluids in her lungs were filling up and basically drowning her, the Lord Jesus reached down and put His hand on her. Just as the Lord did for Paul, *He stood beside her* all the rest of that week and the next and gave her strength. Then after the pastor came in and prayed with her, He allowed her to have dinner with my granddad and my mother. My granddad even got to kiss her goodnight. But, after they left and the nurse was busy, the Lord must have leaned over and whispered, "Nita Ruth, it's time to go home." I believe in her heart she must have said, "Okay," because she did.

God Is My Friend

I am so thankful. You do not know how incredibly thankful I am. During that week and a half, not only did they celebrate my granddad's birthday, but my mother had a wonderful visit with her, and as my mother was staying with my granddad, he wasn't alone when my grandmother died and he received the phone call. Not to mention I can testify to the fact that while I was sobbing and in no shape myself to pray, my spirit inside of me was and God heard me and answered me in a very special way.

In closing, I would like to share a verse with you that a friend of mine just sent me. She knew I had been working on my "friend" chapter and texted me that I should read Psalm 25:14, **"The LORD tells His secrets to those who respect Him; He tells them about His agreement."** The funny thing is that in the Bible translation that was sent to *her*, the verse used the word "friend." But as we were "texting" we looked the verse up in our Bibles and what we read is what I have shared with you.

At first I think she might have been a little disappointed because her initial thought was that it was a friendship verse but after researching, it seems to be a "God sharing secrets" verse. But then it dawned on me, not only was it a friendship verse, it was a deep "best friends" kind of verse. After all, who in the world are you going to share your secrets with but your best friend? So, not only does God want to be friends with us, apparently He wants to be BEST FRIENDS with us, someone He can tell things to, someone He can share things with! How is that for being able to declare *"God is MY FRIEND?"*

In closing of God is My Friend,
♥ __PRAYING IN FAITH__

Father God, we praise You for being such a loving God. Lord, thank You so much for Your friendship and Your willingness to listen to our moans and groans yet love us anyway. Thank You for standing beside us and supporting us. Thank You for showing us this incredible side of You. Thank You also for the testimony that I myself can share.

Lord, I pray that whatever support this reader may need, that You will put Your hand on them, and that they will be able to sense Your friendship with them. Lord God, I pray that one day they also will stand before others and say with assured hearts that "The LORD stood with me."
In Christ Jesus' name I pray,
Amen.

> "Jesus Christ is the same yesterday, today, and forever."
> ~Heb. 13:8~

God Is Stable

When I was a little girl, we lived in West Texas. I was at school out on the playground with some friends when we looked up off in the distance and could see a tornado. We went running to the teacher to tell her, and as she began yelling for everyone to come in, sirens started blaring. The room we went to was an outer room, not part of the main building, and there were doors on either side of the room that our teacher had left open.

I can remember being crouched down—and as one of the ones at the end of the line—I was right by one of the doors leading outside. I can also remember the wind as it ripped through the room and the howling sound it made. My shirt wasn't tucked in and I can even remember the feeling of the wind on my back. Isn't it crazy the things we can remember from when we were kids?

The tornado had ripped our town apart! The hospital was gone; a beautiful row of trees that went down the center of the road I walked down to go to school was completely gone. The whole back patio at our house was removed. Two of the white metal posts were sticking out of our roof. One of our neighbors told us later that they had seen one of our Doberman pups get picked up and tossed into our wooden fence. The strength of that tornado and the destruction it did was incredible. Again, I can still close my eyes and remember what the wind felt like on my back but what I am reminded of even more vividly is that although the tornado had been intensifying, God is even more still.

When the earth shakes, God is still. When the earth trembles and the flood waters roar, God is still. What I mean is: God is still stronger than all of these things. He is the one who causes the earth to shake, but He Himself does not shake. He is sturdy, He is stable.

> **"The LORD is like a strong tower;**
> **those who do right can run to Him for safety"**
> (Prov. 18:10)

However, another verse that gives me something to grasp when I need someone mighty to hold onto is: **"The LORD will roar like a lion from Jerusalem; His loud voice will thunder from that city, and the sky and the earth will shake. But the LORD will be a safe place for His people, a strong place of safety for the people of Israel"** (Joel 3:16).

When we have severe turbulence in our lives, we need to know the God we anchor ourselves to isn't going to buckle. His legs are not going to give out from underneath Him when we go running to Him and all we have time to say is, "Here I am, catch me."

He is our lifeguard and when we are swimming in the sea; He is the one who is on the lookout for us. He can see what is coming at us long before it shows itself to us. When we are in battle and wonder if there will ever be victory because all we can see is the enemy attacking us, God can see the reinforcements just over the hill, for He is the one sending them.

He shelters us and I often think of Jesus stretched out over me like an umbrella. I may be getting a little damp from the sprays here and there, but I can only imagine and be grateful for what He is absorbing with His back! So who am I to complain if I get a little wet? At least I am not getting soaked from the storm. The Lord is taking care of that.

The Very Heart of Worship

God Is Stable

I keep reminding myself that His job is to be God, and my job is to remain in Him. This is easy to do when God is doing what I think He should do, when things are going the way I expected. It is a lot harder when I know I am being obedient, but everything just seems to be going by the wayside! I often wonder if this is how it was for John the Baptist.

One day John was telling people, "I know He (Jesus) is the one, I saw it with my own eyes." John stood up to everyone around him and declared, "This is the man." He believed what God showed him, and he *believed* what God told him. So it is a little heartbreaking when, shortly afterward he was sitting in a cell waiting for death, but praying for help. Day in and day out, no help came, no vindication came, and no release came, no rescue.

Did John succumb to doubt and wonder if he had been wrong? Did he fall to the self-doubt of questioning, "Didn't Jesus know where he (John) was? Didn't Jesus know what was happening?" Yes, John did, because after awhile he sent a message to Jesus asking, **"Are you the one we are waiting for, or is there someone else?"** (Matt. 11:3). And, yes, Jesus did know. He sent a message back to John saying, **"Those who do not stumble in their faith because of Me are blessed"** (Matt.11:6).

It is easy to stand firm in our faith and believe God is stable when what we believe is being played out. When everything we believe is contrary to what we see happening, it leaves room for doubt. But the same thing Jesus told John is what He tells us also. Eventually we will be blessed if we will not stumble in our faith because of what our circumstances look like. At some point we will be rewarded for our faith, if we will believe what God has shown us even when it appears that God has forgotten us or isn't working on our behalf. Know that He hasn't forgotten and He is working.

Basically Jesus told the messengers to tell John that everything was working out the way it was supposed to so not to give up the faith or on what God has said. We have to remember that just like John, even if it appears for us to end in death, we have still won if we can take our faith with us to the death. Because even in death, if we hold to our belief, we still have victory. God is there in death to receive us.

Before I get too far away from the story of the tornado that happened when I was a young girl, I want to share something with you. My grandparents on my dad's side lived in the next town over about 45 minutes from us. The only thing between our town and theirs was a very long West Texas highway.

When it came over my grandparents' radio that our town had been hit by a tornado, my grandfather and uncle jumped in his truck. My grandmother was not about to be left out and took off following my grandfather in her car. About halfway to our town, my grandfather came to a roadblock and was told that due to the destruction no one was being let in until things had settled.

My grandmother, who was behind my grandfather's truck, watched as my grandfather slammed his truck in reverse and backed up, turned the steering wheel, and headed cross-country around the roadblock and kept on going. My grandmother told us later that she sat there for a second and thought, "Okay, well, here we go." And she took out after him. She told my mom and dad later that she thought for sure they were going to jail.

You see, my dad had been out of town. He had been up in the Texas panhandle on a business trip for several days and my mother was home all alone with me and the older of my two younger brothers. So, my grandfather decided nothing was getting in his way or stopping him from getting to us.

The Very Heart of Worship

God Is Stable

Now I share this with you for two reasons: (1) I will admit that whenever I think about this event and my grandfather heading cross-country, it makes me smile and kind of chuckle, and (2) I also share this with you so it will help you to understand how and who my grandfather was. He loved hunting, golfing, and football. But he also had a strong belief in God and loved to sing the old gospel songs. He was stubborn, hardheaded, and loved his family. He was very full of life!

But then the news came one day that he had cancer. It was midlife and he had the rest of his life and retirement to look forward to. During his treatment for cancer he had a stroke. My grandfather did survive the stroke. He even went home, lived with my grandmother for a couple more years, was at my wedding, and lived long enough to see my oldest son after he was born. The problem was—it wasn't my grandfather that came home. Not the one I grew up with. Not the one that went barreling around the roadblock to get to us. This man was quiet and reserved. I still loved him dearly and I know my grandmother was just happy to still have him with her.

But then the cancer really kicked in and with treatment after treatment, he just couldn't win. I learned that it's really hard to grieve for someone who was gone (because the grandfather I knew died in the stroke) but technically was still alive. We had to watch as he slowly suffered and as my grandmother had to step up to fill a role she had never had to before. You see, before the stroke, my grandfather was "THE MAN OF HIS HOME." He was very strong, very dependable, and took care of things. He "wore the pants in the family," that is for sure. And my grandmother loved him. There were times I can remember that she got "spit fire mad at him," but she loved him.

They belonged to a small church in a small town and I know everyone kept praying for him because he still had so much to live for. My grandmother prayed for him and my family prayed for him. But he didn't recover. And my grandmother, who is still alive as I write this, is a very active woman who loves bowling, shopping, golfing, and playing bingo. But she has had to live a number of years without my grandfather. And my grandmother's faith? She has not stumbled!

She still believes that God is good, God is mighty, and that God is God. Some might say her prayers (and our prayers) were not answered. Yet, I know that they were. Maybe not in the way I was hoping, or in the way I know my grandmother was praying. Our prayers just weren't answered on *this* side of heaven. I have no doubt he is home with God. So when skeptics want to say, "God didn't answer your prayers, because your grandfather died." My comment is, "Yes, God did." He answered them in the way He wanted and the way that was best for my grandfather.

Through people in the church and family members, God is taking care of my grandmother. She does miss my grandfather. But when my grandfather was dying and there was nothing that could be done for him, she held onto God, who was a very stable bedrock for her.

A verse our middle son often repeats before saying his bedtime prayers is from Numbers 23:19, **"God is not a human being, and He will not lie. He is not a human, and He does not change His mind. What He says He will do, He does. What He promises, He makes come true."** I like it also. It is good for us to remember that God is not a human and He doesn't have our frailties. He is sure-footed and strong. When storms hit us and we turn to Him, He becomes our rock. He will not be moved; therefore, we shall not be moved.

> **God Is Stable**

One last thing to think about before we end this chapter is from Hebrews 12:26–27:

> **"When He spoke before, His voice shook the earth, but now He has promised, 'Once again I will shake not only the earth but also the heavens.' The words, 'once again' clearly show us that everything that was made—things that can be shaken—will be destroyed. Only the things that cannot be shaken will remain."**

Sometimes God will allow us to be shaken so things that have grown up around us or have become attached to us, that aren't from Him or what He would have for us, will be removed. I like to think about this in terms of a forest fire. The forest can look really full with lots of trees but then a fire comes along and everything that wasn't really alive and was actually dead inside will be removed. But it is in getting rid of the dead growth that new things can grow.

Often this is the only way God can grow us. He lets us go through what seems like fire, where our whole world is shaken, but then afterward we are freed of so much that wasn't really alive, of stuff that on the outside might have appeared to look whole, but God knew better. So He puts us through seasons where everything is shaken but when we come out of it, anything that is *truly of God,* and what God wants for us, will remain with us and in us. We are then able to grow. But keep in mind that during these seasons our world may be shaken, but God isn't and He stays beside us through it until we have reached the other side.

In closing of God is Stable

♥ **PRAYING IN FAITH**

Father God, thank You that Your love for us remains so unchanging and forever lasting. Thank You for all that You do for us and in us. We praise You for Your protection and how often You work things out for us, sometimes without us even being aware of it. Father, You are so awesome to us.

Lord I truly pray for this reader. Father God, may they come to know You so deeply that they also will have a faith and belief in You that will remain unshaken so that no matter what they go through, they themselves will see that You are their stable Almighty God. I praise you, Lord God, because You will be steady even when we are not.
In Christ Jesus' name I pray,
Amen.

> "I am the LORD your God who heals you."
> ~Exod. 15:26~

God Is My Healer

*I*n this look at another name for God, some might be thinking that I am going to talk about physical healing. And though I very much do believe God can and does heal us physically, what I would like to look at in this study is how God heals us emotionally and spiritually.

By the time God took the Israelites to the entrance of the Promised Land, they had been out in the desert for some time. You see, the Israelites needed time with God first. He had things He wanted to teach them, and they needed to be prepared. God needed time to give them new insight as to who He was and to change their perspective and show them how to follow Him and live according to His ways—before entering the Promised Land. Basically, He needed time to clean them up and heal them mentally, emotionally, and spiritually.

God does the same thing to us, and for us. Unfortunately, sometimes this can be painful. As God disciplines us, it can hurt. But so can healing. The problem is that often the person that is going through first discipline, and then healing, can't tell the difference. It's easy to get confused and not be able to tell which is which or to determine which part you are going through at a particular time. I know that many times I have had to stop and ask, *"Okay, God, are You disciplining me for something or are You healing something in me? Because all I know is this HURTS."*

I try to think of the whole "cleansing and healing process" as if I am removing a really deep thorn in my hand. Sometimes you have to dig it out first. And surely there are enough of you out there that know what I am talking about. (Read Ezekiel 36:25–28 when you have some quiet time.)

When our oldest son was in about the third grade, he slid on some rocks at school and hit a stone bench, cutting his head open and requiring stitches. However, by the time I got him to the emergency center, he couldn't walk. The doctor pulled my son's pant leg up to see my son had managed to turn his knee into hamburger meat! The place on his head took three stitches but his knee took a lot more, plus a butterfly bandage on top of the kneecap. Yet before they could even start sewing his knee up, they had to scrub it with something that looked like a toothbrush. Talk about hurting! But it was necessary to clean it out first. And that is exactly what God does to us.

Turn to Second Corinthians 7:10, which says, **"The kind of sorrow God wants makes people change their hearts and live. This leads to salvation, and you cannot be sorry for that."** It goes on to talk about how sorrow caused by worldly things will lead to death, but godly sorrow leads us to want to change our lives. Another verse that describes this process is in Isaiah 30:20: **"The LORD has given you sorrow and hurt like the bread and water you ate every day. He is your teacher, He will not continue to hide from you but you will see your teacher with your own eyes."** Sometimes the only way to get our attention and teach us is to allow us to go through times of suffering.

However, God says if He allows the hurt, or even causes the pain, absolute good will come from it, and He will heal us (see Isaiah 30:26). One of my favorite verses is Isaiah 65:9:

> **"In the same way I will not cause pain without allowing something new to be born,' says the LORD. 'If I cause you the pain, I will not stop you from giving birth to your new nation,' says the LORD."**

God Is My Healer

When I was a little girl if I got in trouble my mother would send me to my room. This was no big deal for me because I could spend hours in there reading, and when the time was over and I could come out, I would actually stay longer. I can tell you whatever my mother might have been hoping to gain or teach was completely lost on me because I didn't mind being in there. That was until my mother caught on.

So, what she would do was to come in my room before shutting the door and remove all my books. Then I felt the punishment! I can remember one time she came in and took every drawer out of my dressers and dumped everything that was in them right in the middle of the floor, everything came out from underneath my bed and everything out of my closet, all into the middle of my room on the floor. Then she told me I couldn't come out until my room was clean.

Now, my mother IS NOT a horrible person, nor is she mean-spirited. So as not to give you the wrong idea, I would like to just say that I love my mother very much. Whenever I bring up this incident at family gatherings, it always turns into a very comical conversation because my brothers will try to top it by saying, "Oh, yeah? Well I remember when I had to...." The problem is that neither my mother nor I can remember what I did to get in so much trouble. I just remember that she did it! She will even chuckle and admit, "Yep, I really did." But, my room got cleaned up and reorganized plus I got rid of a lot of junk. So, all ends well.

The reason I bring this up is because, thanks to this lesson my mother gave me, it has helped me to understand and see that from a spiritual viewpoint God does the same thing in us if we will just let Him. When we finally quit fighting with Him and say, "Here I am, cleanse me," He will clean house and get rid of all the "junk."

When I first came to God as an adult and really surrendered my life to Him I can tell you He came in and cleaned house. I can also tell you that, layer after layer, He scrubbed and cleaned! But boy, let me tell you, it felt so much better after it was done. Early in my walk with God, I kept imagining a particular house. I could close my eyes and just picture the living room. It had beautiful hardwood floors and big tall windows that were open so I could see crystal blue skies through them. Crisp, clean white sheets just billowed out from the breeze coming through the open window. It was clean and immaculate with no furniture. It was wonderful and waiting for someone to move into. Let me tell you, so often I would close my eyes and pray, "Oh, God, please, let me live there. Show me where this house is so I can move there."

After months of what felt like a major construction crew working inside me, suddenly the hammering, cutting, sawing, and drilling that never seemed to quit all just stopped. Sometimes I would look at people and want to ask, "Can't you hear all that?" It was so weird. I could be talking to a friend and visiting with her but inside of me it sounded and felt like a demolition crew was working. But then one day, it ceased. All that was left was quietness and a peacefulness I had never really experienced before. After a while I realized that the house I had been picturing, the big beautiful, clean, clutter-free house, WAS ME. God was cleaning me up, so HE COULD LIVE THERE.

Second Corinthians 1:8–9 says, **"Brothers and sisters, we want you to know about the trouble we suffered in Asia. We had great burdens there that were beyond our own strength. We even gave up hope of living. Truly, in our own hearts we believed we would die. But this happened so we would not trust in ourselves but in God, who raises people from the dead."**

God Is My Healer

My friend, let me tell you, I've been there! The burdens in the soul that feel like you will die from heartache are ones I have endured. But, I can also attest to the fact God really can and does restore you to life. I truly believe this is so we will learn to trust in Him instead of ourselves. I also believe if you are really independent and strong willed, then sometimes the only way God can reach you is to let you get to a point of complete hopelessness.

God cannot fill you up with Him if you are too full of yourself. We have to learn what John taught us in John 3:30, **"He must become greater, and I must become less important."** But somewhere along the way, we have healing.

Here is one last thought before closing this chapter. We have a chain link fence and on the fence is a big, beautiful grapevine. This vine covers the whole fence. It has almost become a privacy fence because the grapevine has grown out so much. But there is one thing missing: there are no grapes. This vine has grown wild for so long in all directions that it has covered the fence. I have to tell you, it's really pretty, with lots of foliage.

But it isn't producing what it is supposed to. The whole purpose of a grapevine is to grow grapes. This one is not. So, if I want it to start doing what a grapevine is intended to do, I am going to have to go and cut some of it down. I am going to have to remove some of the unnecessary branches, clean up some of the limbs, and reposition some of the other limbs so the vine will start growing in the right direction. But why would I do that? Because I can't have it both ways—I can't have a vine-covered privacy fence *and* grapes. I am going to have to choose one or the other.

If you picture yourself as the grapevine growing wild, you can imagine God saying, *"I can't have it both ways. I can't let you continue to grow wild and cover the fence if you are to fulfill your purpose and produce what you are intended and all I have planned. So I am going to have to go and trim you up."* Now the first time I was faced with this, my reaction was, *"WHAT?!"* and *"Isn't that going to HURT?!"* I finally resigned myself to this when God kept insisting, *"I have to."*

What's funny though, is whenever I go through seasons of pruning now, I voluntarily raise my branches! I have learned that, yes, it smarts a little bit, but the end results are so worth it. Also, I have learned that God is a good and loving God and He will only take as long as He absolutely has to and not a second more. Plus, if I don't struggle against Him, it won't hurt nearly as bad and I don't wind up prolonging the process.

Turn to John 15:1–2: **"I am the true vine; my Father is the gardener. He cuts off every branch of mine that does not produce fruit. And He trims and cleans every branch that produces fruit so that it will produce even more fruit."** Verses 1–11 would be something good to read the next time you are having your quiet time with God. Ask God to show you where you may have dead or unnecessary branches in your life that are not from Him and that need to be removed. As He reveals them to you, pray for courage and strength to lift them up to Him so that you can be freed and healed of anything hindering you from producing the fruit intended for you.

Something I would like for us to remember in parting is that God will not do anything that He Himself has not already been willing to do. First Peter 2:24 says, **"Christ carried our sins in His body on the cross so we would stop living for sin and start living for what is right. *And you are healed because of His wounds.*"** (Emphasis mine.)

In closing of God Is My Healer,

♥ **PRAYING IN FAITH**

Father God, thank You that You love us enough to cleanse us and heal us. Thank You for the new heart and spirit that You put in each of us. Lord God, we praise You and thank You that You take the time to minister to us and make us whole again. Father God, I pray that if this reader has any places in them that need healing, that they will lift themselves up to You and feel Your loving hand upon them.
In Christ Jesus' name I pray,
Amen.

> "So Gideon built an altar there to worship the LORD and named it The LORD is Peace. It still stands at Ophrah, where the Abiezrites live."
> ~Judges 6:24~

God Is My Peace

Before starting this chapter, I recently caught myself writing a sentence that read: "One of the amazing attributes about God is...." But really I think everything about God is awesome. From the little birds flying around outside while I sit here working on this to the awesome power of a thunderstorm, and everything in between. From one extreme to the other, what God is capable of is incredible. However, having said that, something that especially overwhelms me is the *peace* He gives inside.

Again, this particular part of our study doesn't come from a specific verse out of our core study passage of Nehemiah 9, but it's more of a deeper thought about something from its timeframe. And that is a look at the peace that God gives His people. Aside from the glow that Moses experienced after spending time in the Lord's presence and the peaceful afterglow Moses enjoyed after he requested, "Show me Your glory," I want to address the peace of heart and peace of mind that God gave Joshua.

When we are introduced to Joshua in Exodus 17, Moses has just put him in charge of the battle campaign against the Amalekites. Now, Joshua could not have been very old because in Exodus 33:11 it says, "**...but Moses' young helper, Joshua son of Nun, did not leave the Tent.**" Nevertheless, this was the man of the hour. So if we turn back to Exodus 17, we read that Moses told him to "go out and fight the Amalekites, but also watch me." Okay, this is where I have to tell you that sometimes I have trouble walking across the room without stumbling over something if I am not paying attention, so the thought of someone telling me to go out and fight a battle but also keep my eye on something else is ridiculous, as I would be a lost cause.

But Joshua was able to do so. He managed to experience victory that even now people still talk about. Why? Because he was watching Moses up on the hill, so in a sense he was watching God. You see, as long as Moses stood on the hill with his hands held up high to the Lord, Joshua was able to win. He knew that the Lord was with them, and he was being assured that the Lord was fighting alongside them. And that kind of blessed assurance will give anyone the peace to fight victoriously.

I tend to think that actually there were two battles going on that day: one down on the battlefield with Joshua leading the way, and a spiritual battle being fought up on the hill. We read that on occasion Moses' hands came down (verse 11). But God gave Moses the help he needed. When it became too hard for Moses to remain standing with his arms in the air, a large rock was placed under him and then when that wasn't enough, his brother Aaron and Hur stood on either side of him helping to lift his arms. When the battle on the ground was over I think Moses—up on the hill—had to have been exhausted mentally and emotionally. But, as long as he could do his part and lift his hands toward the Lord in praise, it gave Joshua the courage to keep going with his part. When you know victory is yours, then the turmoil around you is just the means to an end because there is peace in knowing the battle is already won.

The Very Heart of Worship

God Is My Peace

Years later, after Moses died and it was time for Joshua to step up as leader, the first thing God gave him was more blessed assurance. In Joshua 1:5 it says, **"No one will be able to defeat you all your life. Just as I was with Moses, so I will be with you. I will not leave you or forget you."**

God went on to repeat this three more times to make sure that in his heart Joshua understood that he didn't have to be afraid. If there is no fear, then there is peace inside. And Joshua lived with that for the rest of his life. He followed God, and the Israelites followed him. He lived his life in victory. Make no mistake, there were still battles that had to be fought, a family to save, and land to be conquered and divided but he did it all with God as his mantle.

Would that WE all lived that way. We can, it is possible. Jesus declared it. It says in John 14:27 that, **"I leave you peace; My peace I give you. I do not give it to you as the world does. So don't let your hearts be troubled or afraid."** I love that, "I leave you with peace." Jesus knew what He was about to go through, but He was concerned for His followers. He knew what His death would do to them, so He planted a seed of peace. Ironically, the first time He sees these same followers after His resurrection the first thing He says to them is, "Peace be with you." (See John 20:19.)

Turn to Judges 6:24, where it says that Gideon built an altar and called it, "The LORD is Peace." In the verses covering the time before Gideon was able to build this altar, Gideon had to be convinced it really was the Spirit of the Lord calling on him. I think after the magnitude hit him of what God was commanding him to do and then the realization sunk in that he had seen the Lord face to face, he must have had a fit because the Lord had to calm him down! Look at Judges 6:23, where it says, **"But the LORD said to Gideon, 'Calm down! Don't be afraid! You will not die!'"** Instant peace of heart and peace of mind is evident because immediately Gideon worshiped God.

When I read this, I think of how wonderful and settled he must have felt on the inside and the incredible calm God must have given him. I know many times after I have rebounded from asking God, "You want me to do WHAT?" there has been an overwhelming calmness and assurance, and then all I feel inside is a peace that helps me to say, "Okay, I can do this." And then like Gideon I bow down and give worship to God with all the "thanksgiving in my heart."

Have you ever felt this way: When faced with a difficult situation and from a human perspective you should be a nervous wreck; instead you have a very peaceful and calming presence inside you? My Friend, that would be the peace of God!

When my grandmother died I couldn't go to the funeral so I found myself "puppy sitting" for my brother. When he and his wife got back into town to pick the puppy up, I asked my brother how my grandfather was doing. Any worry I might have had about my grandfather was put to rest with the look on my brother's face. His expression as he thought about my grandfather and then tried to find the words was all I needed. I knew the Lord was standing by my grandfather and was taking care of him so I need not worry.

My brother went on to say after a second of silence, "You know, he was a rock! He was okay." I cannot tell you how much peace that gave me. I truly believe God does that for us. It was not just the comfort I felt, but also the assurance of comfort my grandfather was feeling. It makes me think of Jesus. After hearing that John the Baptist died, all He wanted to do was go off and be alone, but it wasn't to be. Instead, He was descended on by a multitude wanting His help and He (even in His grief) was able to give it.

The Very Heart of Worship

God Is My Peace

At a time when surely He wanted to say, "Not right now, I can't...," He didn't. He cared for the people and gave to them, just like He always did. I really believe God must have been carrying Him that day. I truly believe that when we are emotionally and physically depleted and exhausted and all we can think is, "God, I can't...," that is when He leans down and whispers, "It's okay, I can." And then we find ourselves dealing with difficulties and doing things with such peace and strength that it could not be from ourselves—it can only be from God.

"Blessed assurance" is what I really think Paul was trying to describe in Philippians 4:7, where he says:

> **"And God's peace, which is so great we cannot understand it, will keep your hearts and minds in Christ Jesus."**

And that is truly A GIFT FROM GOD.
In closing,

♥ PRAYING IN FAITH

Father God, how I praise You and thank You that You are so good to us. God, I personally want to thank You for the many times You have given me peace that was so far above understanding. Lord, I just want to pray that if there is any turbulence in this reader's life, that You would pour Your assurance out to them. Reach down and put Your hand on them so that they feel Your calming presence in them.
In Christ Jesus' name I pray,
Amen.

The Very Heart of Worship

> "Trust the LORD with all your heart, and don't depend on your own understanding. Remember the LORD in all you do, and He will give you success."
> ~Prov. 3:5-6~

God Is My Wisdom

When looking at our core chapter of Nehemiah 9, something that occurs to me is that God never left the Israelites. He took care of them and taught them how to live and survive in the wilderness. He didn't give them a whole bunch of rules out of meanness. There was wisdom in what He was telling them. If you go back to the books of Exodus, Numbers, and Deuteronomy, where our core verses originate from, you will see instructions for everything from mold and mildew to eating food that had been out too long. God was concerned for their well-being even if they couldn't see the bigger picture and appreciate it.

During my early 20s I spent two and a half years in Guam. I have to tell you, small island life is a lot different from Austin, Texas, or even West Texas, where I spent most of my time growing up. However, I went prepared. My mother had spent several years in Okinawa as a young girl while my grandfather was in the Air Force.

I grew up hearing about these lizards called geckos that lived in the houses, and large "plate-sized" spiders that didn't crawl but hopped and lived in the trees. Now, I have to admit that when I was little, I thought these stories of my mom's were exaggerated from her youth. Boy, was I wrong! If anything my mother understated all these things.

My first night on the island, I was lying on the floor wondering if I would survive the heat and the smell of fish when I looked up and on the ceiling was a lizard. Then I went into the bathroom and there was one in there also. We had them everywhere so I swallowed and thought, *Please don't tell me there are spiders, too.* The next morning I was outside, and there was a big one. And they really do hop, and sometimes at you!

There are so many more things I could share with you about island living, but seeing how this is a Bible study, I won't go there. However, it is nice to know that if God ever brings me alongside a young military wife going overseas, I could give her a few pointers. In a strange kind of way, this is what God did for the Israelites. Through His wisdom, He taught them how to live.

Turn to Psalm 104:5–9: **"You built the earth on its foundations so it can never be moved. You covered the earth with oceans; the water was above the mountains. But at Your command, the water rushed away. When You thundered Your orders, it hurried away. The mountains rose; the valleys sank. The water went to the places You made for it. You set borders for the seas that they cannot cross, so water will never cover the earth again."**

Dear friend, let me ask you something. If God in all of His infinite wisdom could lay the foundations of the earth, set the stars in the sky, and create our world so that even in unpopulated areas the ground is still watered and the animals are still fed, then isn't it possible that any problem WE might have is something God could handle?

Look at Revelation 1:8, **"The Lord God says, 'I am the Alpha and the Omega. I am the one who is and was and is coming. I am the Almighty.'"** God has been there, He sees all of our tomorrows. He knows what's up ahead of us.

God Is My Wisdom

Tonight I plan on having roast beef for dinner with my family. It's what I am planning and it is only a few hours away. But I know that it is very possible for someone to call me and throw a loop in my plans. I was at work several years ago and got a phone call that our oldest son had just broken his arm and I needed to come home. Let me tell you, I didn't see that coming. But I know God did.

While we are making plans for our lives, let's allow God to be the pilot. Turn to James 4:13–15:

> **"Some of you say, 'Today or tomorrow we will go to some city. We will stay there a year, do business, and make money.' But you do not know what will happen tomorrow! Your life is like a mist. You can see it for a short time, but then it goes away. So you should say, 'If the Lord wants, we will live and do this or that.'"**

If we will put God first in our lives and look to Him each day, then He can and will prepare us for what is ahead. I know so many times before jumping out and doing something, I have waited and just given it some thought and prayed. So often God will change the course of my plans and then later something will come up showing me what I have avoided, and all I can do is say, "Thank You for leading me away from that!"

One morning our youngest son wanted to show me something out behind our house. I had to promise not to open my eyes. He held my hand and led me out of the room, down the hall, through the living room and the dining room, and he made sure I didn't stumble on the step going through the back door while he led me across the patio and then out into the yard under the tree. What he wanted to show me was the water dinosaur park he had made. But, the point is that I never tripped. I never stumbled. He made sure we went very slowly and he talked to me every step of the way. I couldn't see him because my eyes were closed, but I could hear his voice. He was watching out for me, and he did a very good job leading me.

But what amazes me, and the reason I share this with you is that, isn't this what God does? Isn't this exactly what He wants to do for us? We can't see Him, but if we will listen, we will hear His voice. If we will hold His hand, He will guide us. If we are willing, He will walk with us as He promised. Look at Leviticus 26:11-12: **"Also, I will place my Holy Tent among you, and I will not turn away from you. I will walk with you and be your God, and you will be my people."**

Of course, there are stipulations to this so we can't just run wild and do whatever we please. We have to listen to Him and obey what He tells us. But again, don't let the word *obey* scare you. Whatever He tells us REALLY is for our own good. We have to trust Him, also. For instance, we can be traveling on what appears to be a really good path, with no signs of resistance or obstacles, but for some odd reason He tells us to move, or jump over there. What we don't know is what He can see! There could be a sand pit or a dead end leading right over a cliff! We don't know, but we can trust that He does.

It says in Isaiah 30:21, **"If you go the wrong way—to the right or to the left—you will hear a voice behind you saying, 'This is the right way. You should go this way.'"** All we have to do is ask. He will give us the wisdom when we need it. In the same way that each day He gave the Israelites the food they needed for that day, He will give us the wisdom we need each day if we will look to Him for direction. What is amazing is to be able to look back and see over the course of time how He has been already preparing us for something in the future we didn't even know was coming. That is God in all of His infinite wisdom, and He is so willing to share.

In Closing of God is My Wisdom,

♥ **PRAYING IN FAITH**

Father God, we praise You for Your wisdom. God, we praise You because You are so much more aware of everything than we are. Thank You that You lead us, that You direct us, and that You are so willing to walk with us.

God, I continue to pray for this reader. Lord God, I pray that You will give them any wisdom and insight they need, and that You will enlighten them so that they will make it through each day on the path that You would have for them. I also pray that You will help them to hear Your voice and not be distracted by other voices that vie for their attention around them.
In Christ Jesus' name I pray,
Amen.

> "I am God and
> not a human;
> I am the Holy One,
> and I am among you."
> ~Hosea 11:9~

God Is My Companion

If you look back at our core chapter of Nehemiah 9 in either verses 12 or 19, you read that by day there was a pillar of cloud, and by night there was a pillar of fire. God was always present with them. Day or night, He was constantly with them; He never left.

Another verse I would like for you to turn to is Matthew 14:13. After John the Baptist was killed we read, **"When Jesus heard what had happened to John, He left in a boat and went to a lonely place by Himself."** But instead of having the privacy He was seeking, more than five thousand people came looking for Him. Can you imagine needing to mourn but instead being called to help not just a few, but more than five thousand? Yet even in His grief, He felt sorry for them and healed those who were sick and even fed them.

It is amazing how God can work in us and fill us with something we may not even know is there in order to help someone else in need. Here Jesus needed to grieve but hurting people were caving in on Him and somehow He found the strength to do what was necessary. That is the glory of God.

A few years ago my oldest son had broken his arm and wrist in three different places. Yes, he has broken his arm a couple of times. This time he and his best friend decided to master the roof of his friend's dad's shop with a skateboard. When I asked him about gravity and its effects, his comment to me was that they had discussed it and decided they would do a "tuck and roll" when they hit the ground. I don't have to tell you any more about how that worked out for them.

However, the moral to this story is that by the next day my son was in a lot of pain and I was taking him to the doctor. Now I have to tell you, I had a meeting scheduled that evening that I already knew was going to be extremely intense. I was not looking forward to an undeserved verbal confrontation and battering I knew I was going to have to watch a good friend of mine endure so I was really mentally sidetracked.

It's not that I wasn't concerned for our son, but I have to admit between growing up with my younger brothers and raising my three sons (and a few of their very best friends), broken bones are something I have had to learn to deal with. But I was mentally and emotionally upset about the meeting scheduled for that evening and I hadn't slept well for several nights leading up to it, so going to the doctor with my son and trying to be supportive for him wasn't at the top of mind.

But we got through it, and afterward I took my son to get something to eat, and then home. I helped him lay down on the couch as comfortably as I could, but then I had to go back to work. Fortunately, I was self-employed at the time so I didn't have a boss I had to try to please during all this. But I felt so wiped out. There was just nothing left in me, no strength. Then my son texted me so I looked at the phone and it said, "Thanks Mom, you're the best. I love you." Now, I could have sworn that I didn't have it in me. I felt like it was all I could do to be polite through the whole ordeal. But somehow I did. Somewhere in me, without my knowing it, God was working through me to give my son what he needed. I know it had to be God because physically, emotionally, and mentally, I was zapped! But somewhere in me was what my son needed, and it came from God. I truly believe that even without my being aware of it, His presence was with us and it was God, not me, that helped my son.

The Very Heart of Worship

God Is My Companion

If we go back to Matthew 14, we also read that this same evening, Jesus sent the people home and His followers on ahead of Him across the lake. Notice that He still took quiet time alone to pray. But later that night, after He was finished praying, He left to go to the other side of the lake. Now keep in mind that there was a storm. Read Matthew 14:24, **"By this time, the boat was already far away from land. It was being hit by waves, because the wind was blowing against."** Jesus could have skirted around the storm but He didn't. He went straight into it. Why would He do this? Because that's where His friends were, and His place was with them.

I know there are several verses that state that God is with us, but there is one that I don't see much in devotionals that I would like to discuss with you. Please turn to Haggai 2. If you're not familiar with this passage, let me catch you up. Leading up to this, The Lord has said the reason the people of Judah keep working for what seems like nothing is because God was keeping success and blessing from them since they were too concerned for their own homes while His temple still lay in ruins. So Zerubbabel's heart was motivated to rebuild God's temple.

Now this brings us to the verse I want to share, Haggai 2:4–5: **"But the LORD says, 'Zerubbabel, be brave. Also, Joshua son of Jehozadak, the high priest, be brave. And all you people who live in the land, be brave,' says the LORD. 'Work, because I am with you,' says the LORD All-Powerful. I made a promise to you when you came out of Egypt, and my Spirit is still with you. So don't be afraid.'"**

This is something we can always trust about God: when He gives us a job to do, or tells us to go somewhere, we can claim His promise that He will be with us. From God telling Abraham, **"Do not be**

afraid, I will defend you" (Gen. 15:1), to Jesus telling His disciples in Matthew 28:20, **"And I will be with you always even until the end of this age."** God has been comforting His people and telling His people He is with them.

When God gives you the desire to do something for Him, or has given you a specific job to do, know that you can, "Work, because God will be with you." He is your companion, your shadow, your "frontman." Know that Jesus really does "have your back." There is nowhere you can go where God cannot find you or that He won't be able to hear you or reach you.

I love Malachi 3:16, **"Then those who honored the LORD spoke with each other, and the LORD listened and heard them."** When others were spouting off negative remarks about God, some of His people came together to visit about the Lord, and God bent His ear to them and listened. And, when enemy nations talked against God's people and started making plans against them, Scripture says, **"But the LORD was there"** (Ezek. 35:10). Again, when no one was aware of His presence, He was there, He was listening, and He was among them. He is always present. He hears us when we grumble against Him, and He hears us when we complain against Him. But God also hears us when we say good things about Him, when we worship Him, and when we witness for Him. God hears what we say about Him.

So many times in Scripture God says He will go before us, He will fight for us, and that He will give us victory. But also know that during times of trials, when God chooses not to remove the opposition against us, His very Spirit will stand in the fire with us. **"The king said, 'Look! I see four men walking around in the fire. They are not tied up, and they are not burned. The fourth man looks like a son of the gods"** (Dan. 3:25).

The Very Heart of Worship

God Is My Companion

Turn to Isaiah 41:4, **"I, the LORD, am the one. I was here at the beginning and I will be here when all things are finished."** My dear friend, know you are not alone. Take to heart that the Holy One of Israel comes to set the captive free. When you are sitting by yourself and see an amazing sunset or a beautiful blue sky and off in the distance you see a bird just soaring, know that the Sovereign Lord of the universe is by your side. Know He is the one who created what you are seeing. Close your eyes and breathe a sigh of relief that you do not have to do life alone. God meant what He said in Jeremiah 31:3, **"I love you people with a love that will last forever."**

If you ever feel like the whole world is going a hundred miles an hour right past you, and it feels as if you are all alone, know that Christ has been in your shoes. If you go through difficulties and have no one to pray with, know that Christ has been here also. When you find yourself in agony and in prayer it feels as if your heart is ripping, know even there Christ precedes you. Remember Jesus was willing to do what needed to be done, but even still He agonized.

God wouldn't take away what had to be done, but He sent an angel to comfort and strengthen His beloved Son. He sent an angel to do what the disciples failed to do: God gave Jesus someone to see Him through (see Luke 22:43). Dear friend, whether God chooses to fight the battles ahead of us, to remove the obstacles for us, move the mountains in front of us, or stand in the fire with us, know that God promises that through His Son Christ Jesus, we are saved and He has said,

> **"I will never leave you;
> I will never abandon you"**
> (Heb. 13:5).

In closing of God is My Companion

♥ <u>**PRAYING IN FAITH**</u>

Father God, thank You that You are always so near to us. Thank You, LORD that Your love for us is without end. Lord God, we praise You for Your compassion and willingness to forgive us, and that You do so much for us. We praise your name, Holy God of Israel. You are our Lord God and we continue to be amazed by You.

Father God, I continue to pray for this reader and I ask that You will show Yourself to them so that they will feel Your presence close to them and in them.
In Christ Jesus' name I pray,
Amen.

> "Simon Peter answered, 'You are the Christ, the Son of the Living God.'"
> ~Matt. 16:16~

God Is The Living God

When looking at our core study chapter of Nehemiah 9, I always find myself going back and rereading verses 17–21. Only a Living God could have that much compassion and love for a group of people who flip-flopped back and forth between what they believed and worshiped so often.

Those first few years, before they let ten men convince them they couldn't take the land God promised, God did incredible things for them. He constantly showed them amazing things about Himself. He didn't just declare, "I am God, so therefore worship me and do as I say, or else." He could have, but He didn't.

He went above and beyond to teach them so they would know who had delivered them. He gave them every reason to revere Him. But so often they focused on the wrong things and forgot what He had just done for them the day before, and the day before that, and the day before that. Do you ever find yourself doing that? God says, "Child, do you remember what I did before? If I did it then, don't you think I will do it now?"

From the time God clothed Adam and Eve before sending them out into the world and all the way throughout each generation, God has shown us so many attributes of Himself that can only come from a Living God.

I have read the story about Noah's ark many times; I have known about this story since I was a little girl. But one day, not too long ago, I was reading it and something leapt out at me from the Bible version I like to read for my own daily walk. Genesis 6:6 says,

"He was sorry He had made human beings on the earth, and His heart was filled with pain."

Incredibly, the Lord of the universe, the all-powerful Creator, felt pain. It hurts me to think how any of us could live with knowing we caused Him pain, and not know or understand that He is a Living God, not just some supernatural force.

We read that Noah pleased Him and many times throughout Scripture we read God saying He is a jealous God. In reading Scripture, God's Word teaches us that He is merciful, compassionate, and concerned. We read God saying He loves us. If you have never had someone say that to you in all sincerity, then listen with your heart as God says, over and over again in Scripture, "I love you." That can only be spoken by a living creator who, from the beginning of time, has shared His Spirit with us.

My friend, it didn't stop with God; it was passed on in His Son. Turn and read Luke 7:13, **"When the Lord saw her, He felt very sorry for her and said, 'don't cry.'"** In Mark 7:34, we read that Jesus sighed, and in Mark 9:19, we read about Jesus getting frustrated with His followers. These are very real emotions from a very real God. From heartache, disappointment, and sorrow to joy, love, and happiness, there is not a single feeling we can experience that our God cannot relate to. That is one of the reasons I believe He came down as a man. It was so we could relate to Him.

I have been divorced, so I can relate to couples going through very difficult times, but I can also attest to God's healing powers and the rebuilding and new growth God can give us when we have been broken. If you have been through this, or are going through this, I can relate. I know a very dear woman who lost her son when he was only 18. I recently attended a funeral for a mutual friend of ours who lost their 18-year-old son, and though my heart hurt for them and I

> God Is The
> Living God

felt so badly for them, I couldn't relate to their tragedy. I have never personally suffered a loss like this, but my other friend had, so she could relate, and I know that she must have been a source of great comfort to them.

If you grew up without a dad, you will find this in the Bible as well. Paul was a surrogate dad for Timothy. Anything and everything we could possibly go through in our lives has been reflected to us in God's Word, as He has "been there and done that." God is not some "higher power" to keep at arm's length. In James 4, it tells us to "draw near to God." God doesn't want us to be distant relations to Him.

God's Word is also alive; that is why it is so important to read the Bible for ourselves and not just let someone give us a verse here and there or go to church and listen to the sermon but never open our Bible to let God's Holy Spirit work in us. It is in His Spirit who He lives in you.

A man might have held the pen as a vessel, but it was God's Spirit that flowed through him so God's Word could be planted in us and grow. The same message and the teaching of God's Word back then still applies to us today. Jesus said in Matthew 24:35, **"Earth and sky will be destroyed, but the words I have said will never be destroyed."**

God's Word is like living water. When Jesus told Peter to "feed his lambs and sheep," He wasn't just referring to food grown in the field. Jesus was telling Peter to feed people His words, to teach people about Him and feed their souls. When God tells us to feed the hungry, He isn't only telling us to fill their stomachs, He is telling us to feed their spirits, to feed them His words that give life. That's why

He told Joshua to meditate on His words day and night, because they give life.

When Jesus met the woman at the well, His followers were off buying food to fill their physical needs. But when they returned they found Jesus didn't seem so tired and hungry any more, and they mistakenly thought He must have found something to eat while they were gone. But Jesus explained to them that the "food" that had just nourished Him came from doing God's work.

I can witness to this! Several months ago, I was getting sick and had been home most of the day in bed. I think I must have been coming down with the flu, but the bigger problem was that I had an appointment with a gentleman to give him a new Bible and show him how to start a reading plan. You see, he hadn't had a Bible in a while and he and his wife didn't really belong to any particular church. God placed him at my office a few days earlier and after a few minutes he wanted to know how much I would charge for a counseling session. I told him I did not charge to visit about God's Word and boy, the gate opened! He had all kinds of questions, hence the appointment the day I got sick.

And I was not going to cancel it! I just didn't know how I was going to get through it. Two of my sons were home as I was leaving, so they thought they should pray for the appointment. I sat on the coffee table holding their hands while they took turns praying and then I left. I made it to my office, visited with the gentleman, gave him his Bible, and then I went home. All in all I was gone a little over an hour. When I got home, I made an easy dinner for my family, picked up a few things, and then noticed my middle son looking at me funny.

I asked him what he was looking at and his reply shocked me. He asked me, "What happened to being sick with the flu?" After he

> **God Is The Living God**

said that, it occurred to me that although I didn't feel "great," I didn't feel awful either! I had a total burst of energy. I realized it had to have been because of the conversation earlier. It fed me so much to be able to share with someone who was hungry for God. Later that night and then all the next day, the flu hit me like a ton of bricks. But, for just a little while, my spirit was soaring because I had been able to share and witness to someone else who wanted to hear about God.

A verse that has come to mean so much to me is Deuteronomy 8:3: **"He took away your pride when He let you get hungry, then He fed you with manna, which neither you nor your ancestors had ever seen. This was to teach you that a person does not live on bread alone, but by everything the LORD says."**

Sometimes it isn't so much our physical needs that need to be fed as much as it is our spiritual needs. The next time God brings along someone close to you for help, pray and ask God if there are deeper hungers in the person that need to be met. Jesus' call was and still is, "All who are thirsty, come and let them drink." The next time something inside you feels parched, sit down with your Bible and let the Holy Spirit revive you.

In closing of God is The Living God

♥ PRAYING IN FAITH

Father God, thank You for the life Your Word gives us. God, thank You, for Your living water that You so lovingly pour into us. God, help us to absorb Your words. Lord, may they take root inside of us and grow deep in us. Lord, help us to be able to share them with others that You bring alongside of us.

Lord God, I pray for this reader, that the lessons and any help that they may need are being poured into them. God, please keep them and bless them.
In Christ Jesus' name I pray,
Amen.

> "In the beginning You made the earth, and Your hands made the skies. They will be destroyed, but You will remain. They will all wear out like clothes. And, like clothes, You will change them and throw them away. But You never change and Your life will never end."
> ~Ps. 102:25-27~

Section Break III

As we near the end of our journey, I sincerely hope this study has helped you to grow in your walk with the Almighty God. There is so much to learn about our sovereign LORD of the universe. It would be impossible to put into one study the incredible depth of God's love for us and what He willingly does for us every day. There are so many wonderful ways to know God personally. It is my hope that through the course of this study and the 20 names we have looked at, that it has helped to increase your hunger for knowledge of God, which you will later be able to share with someone else.

In starting out in our study, we have seen God is all-powerful, He is all-knowing, and He is faithful. Through our core passage of Nehemiah 9, we see several attributes of God. I hope that you have taken the time to read Nehemiah 9:5–25. If not, then I sincerely encourage you to do so. I suggest you consider taking a couple of different colored pens, read through our core Scriptures, and mark the distinctions you find. Not only can this be very eye-opening, but it also helps to develop a very personal call from God to you. Through our core passage, we learn God starts out by liberating us and then healing us. He goes on to teach us, prepare us for new things, and then,

God delivers us.

> "So God brought His people out with joy, His chosen ones out with singing. He gave them lands of other nations, so they received what others had worked for. This was so they would keep His orders and obey His teachings."
> ~Ps. 105:43-45~

God Is My Deliverer

*I*n preparing for this chapter of our look at different names of God, I prayed and thought long and hard about how God would have me to present this lesson. You see, I am still waiting for some promised deliverances in my life. I can see them coming. Like a storm way off in the distance, the clouds are building and moving toward me. I know the time is almost here. I can almost smell the rain of promised showers in the air.

I have learned there are some journeys that happen relatively quickly. There have been a few occasions where the trip was quick and when God decided to move, it was overnight. I can attest to Isaiah 60:22, **"I am the LORD, and when it is time, I will make these things happen quickly."** When God is ready, my friend, it does not matter what your surroundings may look like or what the circumstances appear to be. When God says, "It's done, I'm ready," _believe Him_! Believe God can raise the dead and that God can call into existence something you would swear is not there. But there have been other trips, other promises of deliverance, promises of new things and growth that have taken *a lot longer* than I ever would have anticipated.

Sometimes I have to remind myself of cooking pot roast. The absolute best way to cook a pot roast is in a crock pot for HOURS. If you want a pot roast to pull apart and melt in your mouth, then you have to let it cook slow and for a long time. Do you know what it is doing while it's in the crock pot all those hours? Being tenderized and prepared. Have you ever noticed that in the first two or three hours, you can raise the lid and see no difference to the outside of the roast? You can check on it after a few hours, and it still looks almost raw, as if nothing has been done to it. In fact, there have been times I have been tempted to turn the heat up and try cooking it a little faster because it looks like it won't be done in time for dinner. But I have learned not to, because it is always done when we sit down to eat. And when my family comes home in the afternoon they can smell it, and they look forward to dinner knowing I have been cooking all day and if they will just give it a little more time, it will be so worth the wait.

My friend, that's us. When we are being prepared for something huge—something life changing—just know we are going to be in the crock pot for hours! But I have come to learn and appreciate that God doesn't do anything half-measure. If you want the very best God has planned for you, then you might as well take a number and sit down because the wait is going to be a while. However, during your waiting time, hold on to past testimonies where God has always delivered on His promises and remember God does not stop until it's done. In the same way that Jesus proclaimed, "It is finished," God does the same thing. He will not stop until you have given birth to what He has promised.

> **"A woman does not give birth before she feels the pain; she does not give birth to a son before the pain starts. No one has ever heard of that happening; no one has ever seen that happen. In the same way no one ever saw a country begin in**

The Very Heart of Worship

God Is My Deliverer

one day; no one has ever heard of a new nation beginning in one moment. But Jerusalem will give birth to her children just as soon as she feels the birth pains. In the same way I will not cause pain without allowing something new to be born,' says the LORD. 'If I cause you the pain, I will not stop you from giving birth to your new nation,' says God" (Isa. 66:7–9).

Dear friend, please know the delivery process can be very painful. It can be very easy to misinterpret labor pains for suffering! Not all pain is because we are being punished for something. Not all pain is indeed suffering. When we are being molded and prepared for something new that we have never done before, know that sometimes God has to redesign us. He has to reshape us and this can be extremely painful if we don't understand what God is doing. So often in this growing process, we don't understand we are being refitted so we start struggling. But in our efforts to free ourselves from the discomfort, we start fighting against the very One who is trying to save us.

When Jesus told Peter to go out in the water for fish, Jesus told him to go out in the *deep* waters. Jesus took Peter out past his head. Friend, I have come to learn that when God wants to take us into something completely new, He will take us to a place where the water is WAY over our heads. But one of the reasons He does this to us is so we learn to trust Him and depend on Him. But, if we start struggling while we are out there, then we are liable to drown!

A few weeks ago, I kept sensing, "Be still." Message after message, devotion after devotion, and lesson after lesson, was "BE STILL." My friend, not every time God says, "Be still," does He mean stop and listen. Sometimes it means, *"QUIT STRUGGLING AGAINST ME."*

I kept having thoughts about a drowning victim. It occurred to me that when someone is drowning and the lifeguard gets to them, the first thing the lifeguard says is, "Be still, quit fighting, or I can't help you."

I finally realized that God had taken me out into some very deep water. (Have I mentioned that I am afraid of water? I love swimming pools because I can see the bottom, but lake water and ocean water terrifies me.) Anyway, I finally realized that I was in a place that scared me, and so I was struggling. I kept getting the message, "Be still." It just took me awhile to understand that God was telling me to calm down! I instantly remembered teaching our youngest son how to float on his back, and I had said the same thing to him!

Sometimes being corrected can be wonderful because with it comes an understanding. You see, I have had three miscarriages and given birth to three babies. And I finally realized the "suffering" I had been going through wasn't really "suffering" at all. God was preparing me for something new in our lives! But, I got confused about the pain. After all, pain is pain, and pain hurts. But the other weekend when God got my full attention, it was as if He leaned down and said, "What part of 'giving birth' do you not remember?" It was such an awesome dawning! As if God was reminding me, "You have given birth to three babies, what part of 'labor and delivery' do you not understand?" I finally realized God was trying to show me that I was right where He wanted me to be—out in some very deep water with Him—and if I didn't stop struggling I was going to drown, and the "baby" right along with me!

I can also share with you that God says NO to drugs. Sorry, but no epidural. When you are being delivered into what God has

The Very Heart of Worship

God Is My Deliverer

promised you or when you are giving birth to something new in your life God has for you, then you have to go through natural birth and you can forget birthing classes. God wants you totally dependent on Him and focused completely on Him. He wants you to rely on His strength, not your own, to get through—to push through.

I think one of the saddest verses I have read recently is from Second Kings 19:3:

> **"They told Isaiah, 'This is what Hezekiah says: Today is a day of sorrow and punishment and disgrace, as when a child should be born, but the mother is not strong enough to give birth to it.'"**

My friend, please don't ever let what God is trying to do for you and through you die because you gave up. My friend, life is hard, delivery is hard, and when God is trying to get you some place and into something new, it can be scary and painful. Sometimes in our fear, we quit because we are too afraid to continue. Sometimes in our weariness, it just seems so much easier to give up. But know this, if you do, then the very thing you have been praying for, hoping for, and waiting for, will very likely die right in front of you.

Dear one, when you reach the point that you just can't push through without an extreme act from God, then pray for God's strength and ask Him to help you break through. I love Second Samuel 5:20, **"So David went to Baal Perazim and defeated the Philistines there. David said, 'Like a flood of water, the LORD has broken through my enemies in front of me.'"**

When I think about being delivered, I often think about orders I had to ship to clients when I had my retail store. I would use FedEx, or sometimes UPS, and I would always look up the tracking information to keep tabs and make sure my clients received what I had sent them. I did not consider it "delivered" until the package had reached the final destination I intended. It didn't matter to me when I looked up the tracking info and saw the package had arrived to the town; it could be driven all over the county, but I didn't consider it "delivered" until it actually reached the destination and person I sent it to. God is the same way with us! We have not been "delivered" until we reach the place God is taking us and would have for us.

Granted, our final place of rest will be in heaven, but while we are here on earth, God has places for us to go and things for us to do. Know that when God delivers us, it will be into something very different. So, if you have been liberated, but it seems like your life is going backward, or downward, or possibly even worse than before you were "set free," then know one of two things has happened. Either you lost your focus on God and have gotten off track or you simply aren't there yet! Trust that God is not going to liberate you and then dump you off in some desert to leave you there.

Yes, things can go downward before being lifted upward. Look at Joseph for just one example. But also know if that is what God has to do with you first, then trust there is a reason and an incredible plan that will affect more than just you. God will not stop until He has prepared you to receive what He has for you. And when the timing is right, once God's plan has been set according to His design, then you also will be delivered. Take heart and hold on to the promise where God says, *"I will do what I said I would do."*

God Is My Deliverer

So, we reach the end of our road, and now we get to celebrate the end of our journey. Turn with me to the last passage in our core study chapter of Nehemiah 9:22–25. After a long and turbulent journey we finally see that after God has liberated His people, taught them, provided for them, healed them, loved them, and kept them, He shows that He is still, and always will be, faithful and His Word is true. Dear friend, we see He delivers them into the very land He has promised. Could they have gotten there sooner? Yes, if they had believed and not turned against Him. Could many of them have made it that didn't? Yes, if they also had listened and not struggled against Him.

But even still, the nation of Israel finally entered their Promised Land. I believe at some point I will also enter mine for I trust that God is faithful. My friend, know in this life there will be storms, but if you will focus on Christ, you also will overcome. Always remember it starts with faith, and it will end in faith. Without faith there is no pleasing God.

Let's read our last core study verses together, shall we?

Part 2: Believing God Is

<u>**Core Study Verses Nehemiah 9:22-25**</u>
**"You gave them kingdoms and nations;
You gave them more land.
They took over the county of Sihon king
of Heshbon and the country of Og king of Bashan.
You made their children as many as the stars in the sky,
and You brought them into the land that You told
their ancestors to enter and take over.
So their children went into the land
and took over. The Canaanites lived there,
but You defeated them for our
ancestors. You handed over to them the Canaanites,
their kings, and the people of the land.
Our ancestors could do what they wanted
with them. They captured strong,
walled cities and fertile land.
They took over houses full of good things,
wells that were already dug,
vineyards, olive trees, and many fruit trees.
They ate until they were full and grew fat;
they enjoyed your great goodness."**

In closing of God is My Deliverer,

♥ <u>**PRAYING IN FAITH**</u>

Father God, we come before You in Christ Jesus' name. Lord, how we thank You and praise You for the wonderful, incredible God that You are. Father God, thank You for this time that we have shared with You, this beloved reader and I. Lord, thank You for teaching us and thank You for shepherding us. Heavenly Father, thank You for all that You do for us and in us.

Lord God, we praise You for being the Lord of our breakthrough. Father God, we pray that the places You would have us to go, the purposes You have created us for, and the plans you have made for us, will all be fulfilled.

Father God, I sincerely hope and pray that this reader will continue to draw close to You and will walk everyday with You. God, I pray that You will be a light to their feet and that You will show them Your way to go. Lord God, I pray that You will show them what steps to take. Please be with them and hold fast to them, as I also pray that they will hold fast to You.
In Christ Jesus' name I pray,
Amen.

The Name of Jesus

"**And the Lord himself will give you a sign: The Virgin will be pregnant. She will have a son, and she will name him Immanuel.**"

~Isa. 7:14~

*O*ne final name I would like to look at and deeply acknowledge is simply the name *LORD JESUS*. You cannot come to the throne of God without first coming to Jesus. You cannot step into the very presence of God without the name of Jesus.

He is the "first born." It doesn't matter if you have siblings or not, or if you are the oldest or the youngest, Jesus is the ultimate BIG BROTHER. If you have ever felt like you never had anyone to watch your back, please know that you do have someone. If you have ever felt like no one cared, or no one would stand up for you, or that no one has ever stood beside you, please know *Jesus is your someone!*

By His stripes we have been forgiven, and because of His death we can be resurrected. Because of His love we have someone to stand beside us, stand up for us, intervene for us, pray for us, and lead us into the very presence of the Almighty God.

If you can't remember any other name in this book, remember the name Jesus. If you get to a place where every thought goes blank, simply pray the name of Jesus. Please turn to Matthew 1 and look at verse 21, **"She will give birth to a son and you will name him Jesus."** (Note: The name *Jesus* means "salvation.")

I absolutely love John 6:37–39: **"The Father gives Me the people who are Mine. Every one of them will come to Me, and I will always accept them. I came down from heaven to do what God wants Me to do, not what I want to do. Here is what the One who sent Me wants Me to do: I must not lose even one whom God gave Me, but I must raise them all on the last day."**

In your heart did you hear that? Jesus said He couldn't and wouldn't lose even one of His people. My friend, know that Jesus has walked into the very pit of hell to reach you, to save you, and to deliver you. He has shown unconditional love for each one of us and the enemy cannot (and WILL NOT) take out of Christ's hand that which belongs to Him.

Jesus said He was "the way, the truth, and the life" and that no one could come to the Father, except through Him. He is the door to eternal life and forgiveness. (Read John 14:1–7.) Jesus told His followers that He and God were one. You can't separate the two. You can't get one without the other. You can't have God without His Son. And Jesus said that if we accepted, loved, and obeyed Him, then He and God would come to live with us. Read John 14:23, **"My Father will love them, and We will come to them and make Our home with them."**

How incredibly awesome is that! Signed, sealed, and delivered with God the Father, Jesus Christ His Son, and the Holy Spirit. We have been bought and paid for, stamped approved, and delivered with an ultimate promise that when we reach our final destination, it will be a heavenly home where God Himself will, **"Wipe away**

every tear from their eyes, and there will be no more death, sadness, crying or pain, because all the old ways are gone" (Rev. 21:4).

If you ever wonder if there will be an end to your heartache, trials, tribulations, and storms, if you ever look at the canyons in your life and wonder how you are going to make it across, if you ever look at the horizon and wonder if the clouds will ever break, or if you ever look out at the darkness of night and wonder if daybreak will ever come, my friend, know that Jesus says, *"I am here, I am the One."*

> **"Jesus, the One who says these things**
> **are true, says, 'Yes, I am coming soon.'**
> **Amen. Come, Lord Jesus!**
> **The grace of the Lord Jesus be with you all.**
> **Amen"**.
> (Rev. 22:20–21)

♥ **PRAYING IN FAITH**

Father God, how we thank You for Your beloved Son, Christ Jesus. Lord, thank You for Your forgiveness which is extended to us through His sacrifice.

Lord God, when I think of the suffering that Christ endured so that we may have everlasting life with you, it is more than my heart can understand. Lord, I pray for this dear reader. Father God, I pray that if they have never personally accepted Your Son as their Savior, that they will today. Father, I also pray that if at one point they have, but their relationship with You has suffered or become distant, then they will bow their heads and renew their commitment to You. Lord God, I pray that even now, they will feel strengthened in You.

Lord, we praise You for Your willingness to forgive, cleanse, and restore us. Thank You that through Christ, we can become new. Thank You that each morning allows us to begin in a fresh way to walk with You. Lord, help each of us to never take that for granted. Father God, bind us to You. Lord, help us not to become distracted by anything that would take our eyes off You. Lord, help us not to forget all that You have done and continue to do for us.
In Christ Jesus' name I pray,
Amen.

♥ *If you have never said a prayer accepting Christ or if you aren't sure where to begin, or maybe it's been a long time and would like to return to Him, then the following leading prayer is for you.*

Prayer for Salvation:

Father God, I come before You. Lord, the Bible says Jesus stands at the door and knocks; and that if anyone hears and opens this door, that He will come in. Lord, I hear You and I am opening the door.

Lord, I open my heart to You and accept Your invitation. Please come in and be Lord in my heart, and Lord of my life. I accept Jesus Christ as my Lord and Savior. I confess to You that I am a sinner, but I ask for Your forgiveness and I ask to be made new. Thank You that I can be washed and cleansed in Christ's blood that He has shed for me so that I may be forgiven.

Father God, for the rest of my life I declare that You are my God and that Jesus Christ is Your Son and that He died on the cross for me. I believe that You resurrected Him and He now lives at Your right hand, and it is in Him that I am set free. Thank You for the grace that You have given me.

Lord, please come in to my life and teach me how to walk with You and live my life for You. Lord, fill me with Your Holy Spirit and make Your home in me until I come to be eternally at home with you.

I praise You, my Father God, and Christ Jesus, my Lord and Savior.
In Christ Jesus' Name,
Amen.

A Worshiper's Heart

"Lord, I will thank You with all my heart; I will sing to You before the gods. I will bow down facing Your holy Temple, and I will thank You for Your love and loyalty. You have made Your name and Your word greater than anything. On the day I called to You, You answered me. You made me strong and brave. Lord, let all the kings of the earth praise You when they hear the words You speak. They will sing about what the LORD has done, because the LORD's glory is great. ~Ps. 138:1–5~

So what is a heart of worship? It is a heart lifted up to God in total adoration of who He is and what He has done for us. It's where our hearts belong—in God. When Jethro, Moses' father-in-law, came to see Moses in Exodus 18, the first thing Moses did was to tell Jethro all God had done for them and what Moses had witnessed. And, *the very first thing* Jethro did was to praise God, and then the two men worshiped in thanksgiving. That's what we should do, that's what we are called to do: to worship God.

When we do this, it takes our eyes off of ourselves and keeps our focus on God, which is where it needs to be. When we worship God, it helps us to see that maybe the whole reason we were able is because God was able. Maybe the whole reason something worked out in our favor is because we are in God's favor. When we are strengthened and have victory, we need to remember where that truly comes from. When we start taking credit, or patting ourselves on the back, we gradually begin to believe in "coincidences" and our eyes begin to close as we completely miss seeing the glory of God.

A heart of worship is a heart that looks toward God no matter what the situation is. *The very first thing* our hearts do is worship the Lord. A heart of worship is a heart that turns to God daily in thanksgiving and spends time in His presence to bask in and to share His love for us. A heart of worship sees past ourselves to the traces of God's movement in our lives, where He has walked with us, worked in us, and gone before us to lead us into all He has for us. A heart of worship seeks God first in all things: in triumph, in victory, in sorrow, in need, in comfort, in friendship, and in complete appreciation and admiration because He is God.

When we walk outside and see a breathtaking view and immediately thank God for His majesty, our heart is in worship. When we watch a loved one do something they could not have done on their own and we know God had to have helped, and quietly thank Him, our heart is in worship. When we are driving and just miss having an accident and, with a sigh of relief, we express thanks to God, our heart is in worship.

When hardship comes and we immediately seek God's counsel, again our heart is in worship. When life falls apart and the first thing we do is ask God, "Where do we go from here?" our heart is in worship. And when things just don't make sense, but we can close our eyes and give it to God by saying, "Your will, not mine," our heart is in worship. When God is all things, when God is our rock, our fortress, our everything, then our heart expresses worship.

Jesus said in John 6:29, **"The only work God wants you to do is believe the one He sent."** If we will just do our part, then God will do the rest. If we will take that one step, God is able to take the rest. If we will do our job, and just trust in Him, obey Him, and worship Him, we will see that LORD *God is GOD.*

Listen to the words of Moses as he sings: **"The LORD gives me strength and makes me sing; He has saved me. He is my God, and I will praise Him. He is the God of my ancestors, and I will honor Him. The LORD is a warrior; the LORD is His name"** (Exod. 15:2–3).

Join with the Psalmist in Psalms 100:3 and rejoice: **"Know that the Lord is God. He made us, and we belong to Him; we are His people, the sheep He tends."**

Let the words in Deut. 4:35–39 go deep into the recesses of your heart: **"You were shown these things so that you might know that the LORD is God; besides Him there is no other. From heaven He made you hear His voice to discipline you. On earth He showed you His great fire, and you heard His words from out of the fire. Because He loved your ancestors and chose their descendants after them, He brought you out of Egypt by His Presence and His great strength, to drive out before you nations greater and stronger than you and to bring you into their land to give it to you for your inheritance, as it is today. Acknowledge and take to heart this day that the LORD is God in heaven above and on the earth below. There is no other."**

And then listen to the mightiness of the Voice of God saying:

> "I am the Lord. That is My name.
> I will not give My glory to another;
> I will not let idols take the praise that should be mine."
> (Isa. 42:8)

Part 2: Believing God Is

**Take heart today, simply KNOW and BELIEVE that the LORD Is God—He is *YOUR* GOD!
Know that the LORD is His name, He waits for you to call upon Him, and He waits for you to personally *"come and see"* and get to know Him.**

♥♥♥♥♥♥♥♥♥♥♥♥♥♥♥♥♥♥♥♥♥♥♥♥♥♥♥

My dear friend, as I close this chapter and this section of looking at the names of God that we have studied, I sincerely hope that by sharing some of my experiences with you, it will help and encourage you to look for and see traces of God's handprints in your life. I truly pray that by sharing some of my testimonies with you, it will help to strengthen your walk and relationship with God. I pray for you, my thoughts are with you, and may God bless you.

Sincerely,
Your Friend in Christ,
Kassie

♥ Praying In Faith
of Thanksgiving and Praise to the LORD Our God

> "Everything on earth, shout with joy to God! Sing about His glory! Make His praises glorious! Say to God, 'Your works are amazing! Because Your power is great, Your enemies fall before You. All the earth worships You and sings praises to You. They sing praises to Your name.'"
> ~Ps. 66:1–4~

Lord, we praise You, for You are the One who stirs up the sea and makes the waves roar. We praise You, by the name You call Yourself, the All-Mighty God. You are all-knowing, and we are so thankful that nothing can come to us without Your knowledge. God, we praise You for being faithful. We thank You that You keep Your agreement of love for a thousand lifetimes for people who love You and obey Your commands.

Thank You for being our liberator and for the freedom You give us from so many things. God, we praise You because Your Word promises us that You will not let us be defeated. We praise You, the One who guards us. Thank You for leading us as we go along paths that we have not known before. Thank You for changing the darkness into light. Thank You for Your promise not to leave us. God, we praise You for Your counsel given to us. God, thank You for the provisions that You give us and the loyalty You show us.

Lord God, we praise You for being our teacher and for how good You are to us. We praise You for the truth we find in Your Words. Thank You for being our friend. And thank You for Your Holy Spirit who helps us to know what You would say to us. God, we praise You because You do not change. The same God you were to Abraham, Isaac, and Jacob is who You are to us now.

Thank You for healing us and for the peace You give us in our hearts. Father God, thank You for Your wisdom and for the fact that we don't have to lean on our own understanding because You promise to give us direction. Lord God, we praise You because with You we know that we are not alone and that You are among us even when we are unaware of it.

Father God, thank You for Your Son, who died on the cross for us and through Him for the forgiveness You give us. Father, we claim Him as Your Son, the Son of our living God. Lord, thank You for the deliverance that You have given us. Thank You for bringing us to a place with You and in You where we can have joy and thanksgiving. Thank You, that when You liberate us, You also cleanse us and prepare us for the blessing You bestow upon us.
In Christ's Name,
Amen

Part 3: Study Reference

The following section includes:

- Names of God, memory verses to meditate on
- Core Study Guide Passage of Nehemiah 9:5–25

Nehemiah 9:5–25 represents our core study chapter while looking at different names that God gives us to call Him in part 2 of this book. Throughout this study, we will look at many different parts of the Bible, but this is the main passage we will continue to look back at as a reference point. I encourage you to bookmark this chapter in your personal Bible so that it will be easier for you to go back and forth to during this study.

Please note: the following study guide (included here for you) is in the New Century Version, which is the version we've used throughout this study. However, I encourage you to read Nehemiah 9 in several different versions, as your study time allows. I have found that often times reading the same passage in different versions periodically will open up our minds, enabling God to give us fresh insight and deeper encounters into His Word.

Part 3: Study References

Names of God Memory Verses

God Is: My Provider (Gen. 22:14):
"So Abraham named that place The LORD Provides.
Even today people say
'On the mountain of the LORD it will be provided.'"

God Is: Loyal (Zech. 8:8)
"I will bring them back, and they will live in Jerusalem.
They will be My people, and I will be their good and loyal God."

God Is: My Teacher (Hosea 12:10)
"I spoke to the prophets and gave them many visions,
Through them, I taught my lessons to you."

God Is: Good (Ps. 136:1)
"Give thanks to the LORD because He is good.
His love continues forever."

God Is: Truth (Ps. 33:4–5)
"God's word is true, and everything He does is right.
He loves what is right and fair; the LORD'S love fills the earth."

God Is: My Friend (John 15:15)
"I no longer call you servants, because a servant
does not know what his master is doing. But I call you friends,
because I have made known to
you everything I heard from My Father."

God Is: Stable (Heb. 13:- 8)
"Jesus Christ is the same yesterday, today, and forever."

God Is: My Healer (Exod. 15:26)
"I am the LORD your God who heals you."

God Is: My Peace (Judg. 6:24)
"So Gideon built an altar there to worship the LORD and named it The LORD Is Peace. It still stands at Ophrah, where the Abiezrites live."

God Is: My Wisdom (Prov. 3:5–6)
"Trust the LORD with all your heart, and don't depend on your own understanding. Remember the LORD in all you do, and He will give you success."

God Is: My Companion (Hosea 11:9)
"I am God and not a human; I am the Holy One, and I am among you."

God Is: The Living God (Matt. 16:16)
"Simon Peter answered, 'You are the Christ, the Son of the Living God.'"

God Is: My Deliverer (Ps. 105:43–45)
"So God brought His people out with joy, His chosen ones out with singing. He gave them lands of other nations, so they received what others had worked for. This was so they would keep His orders and obey His teachings."

God loves you, God cares for you,
and God has said you are His people.
God is willing, God is able,
and God is waiting.
Whoever you need God to be for you,

GOD IS.

Part 3: Study References

Core Study Chapter Nehemiah. 9:5–25

5 "Blessed be your wonderful name. It is more wonderful than all blessing and praise."

6 "You are the only Lord. You made the heavens, even the highest heavens, with all the stars. You made the earth and everything on it, the seas and everything in them; You give life to everything. The heavenly army worships you."

7 "You are the Lord, the God who chose Abram and brought him out of Ur in Babylonia and named him Abraham."

8 "You found him faithful to you, so you made an agreement with him to give his descendants the land of the Canaanites, Hittites, Amorites, Perizzites, Jebusites, and Girgashites. You have kept Your promise, because You do what is right."

9 "You saw our ancestors suffering in Egypt and heard them cry out at the Red Sea."

10 "You did signs and miracles against the king of Egypt, and against all his officers and all his people, because You knew how proud they were. You became as famous as You are today."

11 "You divided the sea in front of our ancestors; they walked through on dry ground. But You threw the people chasing them into the deep water, like a stone thrown into mighty waters."

12 "You led our ancestors with a pillar of cloud by day and with a pillar of fire at night. It lit the way they were supposed to go."

13 "You came down to Mount Sinai and spoke from heaven to our ancestors You gave them fair rules and true teachings, good orders and commands."

14 "You told them about Your holy Sabbath and gave them commands, orders, and teachings through Your servant Moses."

15 "When they were hungry, You gave them bread from heaven. When they were thirsty, You brought them water from the rock. You told them to enter and take over the land You had promised to give them."

16 "But our ancestors were proud and stubborn and did not obey Your commands."

17 "They refused to listen; they forgot the miracles You did for them. So they became stubborn and turned against You, choosing a leader to take them back to slavery. But You are a forgiving God. You are kind and full of mercy. You do not become angry quickly, and You have great love. So You did not leave them."

18 "Our ancestors even made an idol of a calf for themselves. They said, 'This is your god, Israel, who brought you up out of Egypt.' They spoke against You."

19 "You have great mercy, so You did not leave them in the desert. The pillar of cloud guided them by day, and the pillar of fire led them at night, lighting the way they were to go."

20 "You gave your good Spirit to teach them. You gave them manna to eat and water when they were thirsty."

21 "You took care of them for forty years in the desert; they needed nothing. Their clothes did not wear out, and their feet did not swell."

₂₂ "You gave them kingdoms and nations; You gave them more land. They took over the country of Sihon king of Heshbon and the country of Og king of Bashan."

₂₃ "You made their children as many as the stars in the sky, and You brought them into the land that You told their ancestors to enter and take over."

₂₄ "So their children went into the land and took over. The Canaanites lived there, but You defeated them for our ancestors. You handed over to them the Canaanites, their kings, and the people of the land. Our ancestors could do what they wanted with them."

₂₅ "They captured strong, walled cities and fertile land. They took over houses full of good things, wells that were already dug, vineyards, olive trees, and many fruit trees. They ate until they were full and grew fat; they enjoyed Your great goodness."

Closing Prayer

Father God,

Thank You. Thank You for this journey You have taken us on, thank You for Your words that You have taught us and given us. Lord God, I pray for this reader who has shared in this study with me. God, thank You for this opportunity that we have had to come together to learn about You.

God, I sincerely pray for them and about them. Lord, I don't know what their name is, or where they come from, but I know that You do, so I pray that through You they will know that I fully pray blessing for them from You. Lord, I pray that they will come to know You more and that their personal relationship with You will grow. Lord, I pray that this reader will come to know what You would have for them. I pray that You will bless them with greater wisdom and understanding in spiritual things so that they can and will live the kind of life that honors and pleases You in every way. I pray that they will produce fruit in every good work and will continue to grow in their knowledge of You.

Lord God, please strengthen them with Your great power so that when troubles come, they will be patient and not give up. Help them to always remember to give joyful thanks in all that You allow them to be a part of in the growing of Your kingdom. Lord, thank You for freeing them from the powers of darkness and bringing them into Your glorious light.

Father God, may You bless them and keep them. Please show Your kindness and mercy on them. Lord, I ask You to watch over them and give them peace as they look to You, the Awesome and Sovereign Lord of the universe.

In the Mighty Name of Christ Jesus, our Lord and Savior,
Amen.

About Cypress Ministries

and Making JESUS' NAME Known

"For I proclaim the name of the Lord: ascribe greatness to our God. He is the Rock, His work is perfect; for all His ways are justice, a God of truth and without injustice; righteous and upright is He" (Deut. 32:1-4 NKJV).

First and foremost, we seek with all our hearts, to honor and glorify God with our lives in all that we do. It isn't about making us known, but to make HIM known. We have a deep desire to help others who are seeking to grow in their daily walk with God, while learning to listen to the leading of God's Holy Spirit; and simply coming to know God, to believe what He says and to worship Him, because He Is God.

> *Following in God's direction, and the Pathway of Faith to spiritual health and healing.*

Cypress Ministries is the writing and leadership ministry of the Pathway of Faith foundation. Our main focus is on feeding those who are hungry (and thirsty) for a deeper relationship with God the Father (and the Way of Christ), through the teaching of His Word. Though our primary call is to "feed God's people" we have a deep burden as well, to bring a message of HOPE to the brokenhearted and downcast, to show them that all is NOT lost, and that through Jesus Christ there IS spiritual health and healing, and eternal life.

About This Book

The Very Heart of Worship is the **core** book and study of
A Worshiper's Heart Bible Study Series
Written by Cypress Ministries

Also available is The Very Heart of Worship;
Personal Study Guide—Special Edition.

We also invite you to check out the companion notebook for this series called **Knowing and Believing Who God Is.** (This notebook works with either edition of The Very Heart of Worship.)

Other future books that will be included in this series:
- A Heart of Faith
- A Heart of Praise
- Maintaining a Believing Heart

For more information on this Bible study series, please visit:
www.aworshipersheart.com

♥♥♥♥♥♥♥♥♥♥♥♥

We sincerely pray that the message we hope to express in this book has been insightful to you and has helped to deepen your relationship with God, His Son, and the Holy Spirit.

In following Jesus' example, we are searching for God's lost people, ministering to the disappointed, the hurt, and the lonely, and gently reminding them that Jesus is the way.

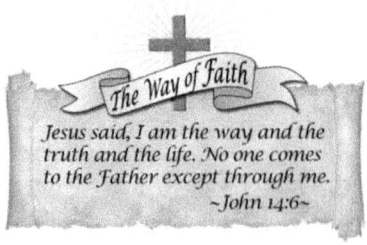

The Way of Faith
Jesus said, I am the way and the truth and the life. No one comes to the Father except through me.
~John 14:6~

http://www.cypressministries.com

www.ingramcontent.com/pod-product-compliance
Lightning Source LLC
Chambersburg PA
CBHW071311110426
42743CB00042B/1270